FUN, FITNESS, AND SKILLS

The Powerful Original Games Approach

Howie Weiss

Human Kinetics

Library of Congress Cataloging-In-Publication Data

Weiss, Howie, 1944-
 Fun, fitness, and skills : the powerful original games approach / Howie Weiss.
   p. cm.
 ISBN-13: 978-0-7360-6829-1 (soft cover)
 ISBN-10: 0-7360-6829-5 (soft cover)
 1. Physical education and training--Study and teaching. 2. Physical fitness for children-
-Study and teaching. 3. Group games. I. Title.
 GV361.W36 2008
 372.86--dc22

                                        2007028579

ISBN-10: 0-7360-6829-5
ISBN-13: 978-0-7360-6829-1

Copyright © 2008 by Howie Weiss

Acquisitions Editor: Scott Wikgren; **Developmental Editor:** Ragen E. Sanner; **Assistant Editor:** Anne Rumery; **Copyeditor:** Kathy K. Calder; **Proofreader:** Julie Marx Goodreau; **Graphic Designer:** Fred Starbird; **Graphic Artist:** Dawn Sills; **Photo Manager:** Laura Fitch; **Cover Designer:** Keith Blomberg; **Photographer (cover):** © Human Kinetics; **Photographer (interior):** © Human Kinetics; **Art Manager:** Kelly Hendren; **Assistant Art Manager:** Alan L. Wilborn; **Illustrator:** Alan L. Wilborn; **Printer:** Versa Press

Printed in the United States of America   10   9   8   7   6   5   4   3   2   1

Human Kinetics
Web site: www.HumanKinetics.com

United States: Human Kinetics
P.O. Box 5076
Champaign, IL 61825-5076
800-747-4457
e-mail: humank@hkusa.com

Canada: Human Kinetics
475 Devonshire Road Unit 100
Windsor, ON N8Y 2L5
800-465-7301 (in Canada only)
e-mail: orders@hkcanada.com

Europe: Human Kinetics
107 Bradford Road
Stanningley
Leeds LS28 6AT, United Kingdom
+44 (0) 113 255 5665
e-mail: hk@hkeurope.com

Australia: Human Kinetics
57A Price Avenue
Lower Mitcham, South Australia 5062
08 8372 0999
e-mail: info@hkaustralia.com

New Zealand: Human Kinetics
Division of Sports Distributors NZ Ltd.
P.O. Box 300 226 Albany
North Shore City
Auckland
0064 9 448 1207
e-mail: info@humankinetics.co.nz

To my wife Elaine and my children Irene and Sharon, who always encouraged and stood by me.

I also dedicate this book to the New York City school students who were kind enough to play these games until they were perfected.

Contents

Game Finder

Game title	Page number	Ages	Aerobic endurance	Muscular strength and endurance	Flexibility	Locomotor skills	Manipulative skills	Social skills	Curricular and thinking skills	Safety awareness	Holiday games
										Topic	
Chapter 2 Warm-Ups											
Dance Challenge	6	7+	✓			✓		✓			
Everybody's It	7	7+	✓			✓		✓			
Freedom Fighters	8	7+	✓	✓		✓	✓				
Get Set	9	4+	✓					✓	✓		
How Many?	10	6+	✓	✓	✓				✓		
Is It Time Yet?	11	5+	✓						✓		
Partner Ball	12	7+	✓				✓				
Partner Fitness	13	8+		✓							
Partner Tag	14	7+	✓					✓			
Psychic Warm-Up	15	5+	✓	✓	✓	✓					
Read and Do	16	5+	✓			✓			✓		
Reading Exchange	17	6+	✓			✓		✓	✓		
There, Their, and They're	18	8+	✓			✓			✓		

Game title	Page number	Ages	Aerobic endurance	Muscular strength and endurance	Flexibility	Locomotor skills	Manipulative skills	Social skills	Curricular and thinking skills	Safety awareness	Holiday games
Chapter 3 Fitness Games											
April Fools' Hunt	20	6+	✓	✓	✓	✓		✓			✓
Ball Exchange	22	8+	✓			✓	✓	✓			
Bowlers and Setters	24	7+	✓				✓	✓			
Cardio Obstacle Course	26	8+	✓	✓		✓	✓	✓			
Collection	28	8+	✓			✓	✓	✓			
Concentration	30	7+	✓			✓	✓				
Cooperative Catch	32	8+	✓			✓	✓	✓			
Crossfire	34	8+	✓				✓	✓			
Egg Soccer	36	8+	✓				✓	✓		✓	✓
Figure It Out	38	4+	✓			✓	✓	✓			
Fitness Ball	40	7+	✓				✓	✓		✓	
Fitness Exchange	41	8+	✓	✓	✓	✓	✓				
Fitness Feud	43	5+	✓			✓	✓				
Fitness Island	44	5+	✓	✓		✓		✓	✓	✓	
Fitness Run	48	8+	✓	✓	✓	✓			✓		
Follow the Leader	50	4+	✓			✓	✓	✓		✓	

(continued)

(continued)

Game title	Page number	Ages	Aerobic endurance	Muscular strength and endurance	Flexibility	Locomotor skills	Manipulative skills	Social skills	Curricular and thinking skills	Safety awareness	Holiday games
					Topic						
Chapter 3 Fitness Games *(continued)*											
Gym Scooter Derby	51	4+	✓	✓				✓		✓	
Keep-Away Scooter Ball	53	8+		✓			✓				
Movement Partners	54	5+	✓			✓		✓			
No-Relay Relay	56	5+	✓	✓		✓	✓	✓			
Now	58	8+	✓			✓	✓	✓		✓	
Partner Scooters	60	8+	✓	✓			✓	✓			
Return the Fitness Favor	61	8+	✓	✓			✓	✓	✓		
Scrabble Fitness	63	5+	✓					✓	✓		
Spaghetti, Spaghetti, Meatball Parachute	65	4+		✓		✓		✓			
Trick or Treat	67	7+	✓	✓			✓	✓			✓
Wheelbarrow Challenge	69	8+		✓		✓		✓			
Zombie Ball	71	8+	✓			✓	✓	✓			✓
Chapter 4 Tag Games											
Alien Remedy Tag	75	5+	✓			✓	✓	✓		✓	
Basketball Dribble Tag	77	8+	✓			✓	✓	✓			

Game title	Page number	Ages	Aerobic endurance	Muscular strength and endurance	Flexibility	Locomotor skills	Manipulative skills	Social skills	Curricular and thinking skills	Safety awareness	Holiday games
Basketball Knock Away	79	8+	✓				✓	✓		✓	
Basketball Shoot and Tag	80	8+	✓				✓	✓			
Beanbag Tag	82	5+	✓			✓	✓	✓			
Bowling Pin Tag	84	6+	✓			✓	✓	✓			
Cranky Crab Tag	86	5+		✓		✓		✓			
Domino Tag	87	5+	✓			✓		✓		✓	
Endangered Species Tag	89	7+	✓			✓		✓	✓	✓	
Gymnastic Tag	90	8+	✓	✓				✓		✓	
Hoop Tag	93	7+	✓			✓	✓	✓		✓	
Monster Tag	95	5-7	✓			✓		✓		✓	✓
Moving Duck Duck Goose	96	5-10	✓			✓		✓			
Mystery Tag	98	5+	✓			✓	✓	✓		✓	
Pokemon Tag	99	7-10	✓			✓		✓			
Quest for Freedom Tag	101	8+	✓			✓	✓	✓		✓	
Secret Santa Tag	104	6+	✓			✓				✓	✓
Soccer Tag	105	7+	✓				✓	✓			
Sports Tag	107	8+	✓			✓	✓	✓			

(continued)

(continued)

Game title	Page number	Ages	Aerobic endurance	Muscular strength and endurance	Flexibility	Locomotor skills	Manipulative skills	Social skills	Curricular and thinking skills	Safety awareness	Holiday games
							Topic				
Chapter 4 Tag Games *(continued)*											
Thanksgiving Feast	108	7+	✓			✓		✓	✓		✓
Turkey Tag	111	5+	✓			✓	✓	✓		✓	✓
Chapter 5 Fitness Games With a Skill Emphasis											
1-2-3 Ball	114	8+	✓				✓	✓			
America Online Ball	115	8+	✓				✓	✓			
Basketball Around the World	117	8+	✓				✓	✓			
Basketball Concentration	118	8+	✓				✓			✓	
Basketball Music Pass	120	8+	✓			✓	✓	✓			
Bingo Ball	121	8+	✓				✓	✓		✓	
Bowling Pin Soccer	124	8+	✓	✓			✓	✓			
Chinese Checkers	125	8+	✓				✓	✓			
Cooperative Partners	127	5-7	✓				✓	✓			
Desert Island Volleyball	128	6+	✓				✓	✓			
Dispatcher	131	8+	✓					✓			
Down the Chimney	133	5+	✓				✓	✓			✓
Elves Versus Grinches	135	8+	✓				✓	✓	✓		✓

Game title	Page number	Ages	Topic								
			Aerobic endurance	Muscular strength and endurance	Flexibility	Locomotor skills	Manipulative skills	Social skills	Curricular and thinking skills	Safety awareness	Holiday games
Fearsome Five	137	8+	✓				✓			✓	
Ice Cream Cones	139	5+	✓			✓	✓	✓			
Multiple Partners	140	5+	✓	✓	✓		✓	✓			
Pirate Ball	143	8+	✓				✓	✓		✓	
Quick Partners	145	5+	✓			✓		✓			
Soccer Bump	146	8+	✓				✓	✓			
Titanic	148	8+	✓				✓	✓			
Turn Off the TV	150	7+	✓	✓		✓	✓	✓	✓		
Vampire Ball	152	8+	✓				✓	✓			✓
Chapter 6			**Games for Students Ages Four to Seven**								
Abracadabra	156	4-7	✓			✓					
Alphabet Soup	157	4-7	✓			✓		✓	✓		
Camouflage	159	4-7	✓			✓		✓			
Far Away	161	4-7	✓					✓		✓	
Fast Partners	162	4-7	✓			✓		✓		✓	
I'm Tired	163	4-7	✓			✓		✓		✓	
Letter Cones	165	4-7	✓			✓		✓	✓	✓	
Progressive Movement	166	4-7	✓			✓				✓	
Stay in the Boat	168	4-7	✓			✓		✓			

Preface

The idea for *Fun, Fitness, and Skills: The Powerful Original Games Approach* came from my own desire to make skill development and fitness education as much fun as possible for all students, as well as for myself. How often do students and teachers become bored by constantly using the same games and drills? Of course, one can search the Internet or look at game books. I have found nearly all of these books and lesson plans repetitive, merely recycling old ideas. So I have put my 30-plus years of experience to use, creating new and exciting games and offering exceptional teaching and classroom management suggestions.

The material in *Fun, Fitness, and Skills: The Powerful Original Games Approach* will significantly improve your teaching ability. The number of games is endless, because each game has so many variations and possibilities. These variations will enable you to easily adjust the games to all age and ability levels. When teaching any sport or activity, you may use many of these games by simply changing equipment and modifying one or two rules. Several of the games utilize fantasy, holidays, movies, familiar games with a new twist, TV shows, and other connections to the world students live in. Most of the games are cooperative in nature, but they have a low-key competitive element or variation as well. Physical education teachers (elementary through high school), program directors, recreational specialists, classroom teachers, and coaches will discover exciting new ways to teach or improve their students' skills and fitness.

The book's introduction explains the purpose and format of *Fun, Fitness, and Skills: The Powerful Original Games Approach.* The Game Finder allows you to quickly find a game that matches your objective and the age you wish to teach. However, because each game has multiple variations, you will actually be able to address any topic, ability, or age by making one or more small modifications. Chapter 1 helps you become an expert in teaching games. Chapter 2 gives you some new dynamic warm-ups. Chapter 3 focuses on health-related fitness but also includes skill-related fitness and skill practice for various sports. Chapter 4 contains fun original tag games with an explanation of the many different formats these games can take. Chapter 5 focuses on sports and on skill-related fitness but still contains a health-related fitness component. Chapter 6 describes games designed specifically for young children, ages four to seven. These are great fitness games that help teach locomotor skills and spatial awareness. Finally, chapter 7 provides the tools necessary for you and your students to create your own original games.

The current emphasis on Physical Best and on Fitnessgram makes this book a vital partner in encouraging all children to become more active now and seek activities they can enjoy for life. New York City physical education teachers have been asking for new ways to help their students develop a healthy lifestyle. My current job as a physical education mentor and staff developer with the Department of Education in New York City provided me the opportunity to field-test these games in many kinds of schools with diverse student populations and on many different grade levels. The games have been met with resounding success. The students have found them to be great fun. The teachers have found them education-ally sound and easy to follow. Just turn the page and immerse yourself in the world of truly imaginative *Fun, Fitness, and Skills: The Powerful Original Games Approach.*

Introduction

Fun, Fitness, and Skills: The Powerful Original Games Approach allows students of all abilities to work together by offering numerous choices and variations. These enormously enjoyable games combine skill and fitness instruction with practice. Every game is uniquely crafted to utilize diverse approaches to learning while maximizing physical and mental activity. Students can play most games either cooperatively or competitively. When they play the competitive alternative, the competition is not overt. The games aim to eliminate students' anxiety about participating in games and their complaints about practicing boring drills. *Fun, Fitness, and Skills: The Powerful Original Games Approach* provides the tools for education while creating the fun to keep every student begging for more.

Whether to play a game, practice a skill, or work on physical fitness is a choice that most physical education teachers face every day. Children need to practice in order to improve, but they quickly become bored with ordinary drills. Teachers know that children would much prefer to play games, but they also know that many of the students are ill-prepared to play those games. Additionally, when playing modified games, some of the skilled children want expanded opportunities to demonstrate their abilities. The skill practices, drills, or modified games often lead to discipline problems or to students displaying very little effort. When placed in game situations, many children become unhappy, confused, or anxious because they do not have the skill or knowledge to play the game. The skilled players tend to dominate games, leaving the unskilled to stand around, seek excuses to remove themselves from what they perceive as a hostile environment, and expose themselves and others to injury. By playing games that are specifically geared to teaching skills and promoting fitness, you promote game playing, skill building, and fitness building at the same time. Many of the variations in *Fun, Fitness, and Skills: The Powerful Original Games Approach* allow the more naturally athletic or competitive students to enjoy play, while not publicly exposing the less athletic or less competitive students' weaknesses.

Fun, Fitness, and Skills: The Powerful Original Games Approach contains game formats that allow you, the teacher, to move around and teach while actually differentiating instruction. In the activities you never act just as a scorekeeper or referee. The games allow you to do all of the following:

- Respect the readiness level of each student for such things as ball choice, strike type (set, pass, or spike), distance traveled with each strike, and travel speed
- Offer advice to all students to improve growth (by walking around to each pair or group)
- Escalate the degree of difficulty as students develop skills (changing partners or groups or performing more difficult skills)
- Assess in an ongoing and diagnostic manner

Each game described will easily adapt to, or constitute in itself, a complete lesson plan. By changing the equipment or skill emphasis, you can adapt many games to multiple sports and to life activities. The games are written so that they help teachers meet National Association for Sport and Physical Education (NASPE) standards as well as local or state standards. Desert Island Volleyball in chapter 5, page 128, shows how to incorporate the national standards into your lesson plans.

Game descriptions include these sections:

- Ages—Designates ages that are typically developmentally appropriate for the game. You can adjust these suggested age levels according to your students' abilities.
- Topics—Lists skills and fitness areas that the game addresses.
- Objectives—Identifies the psychomotor, cognitive, and affective goals that a teacher can address by using the game.
- Equipment—Lists the type and amount of equipment needed for the game.
- Safety—Notes any safety concerns to be aware of or share with students.
- Game—States the procedures for the game.
- Variations—Lists the many ways to vary the game to meet other needs and skill levels.

Be sure to read chapter 1 carefully before playing the games in this book. This chapter will make it easy for you to understand how to teach and play the original games. After playing a number of them, you will be able to create your own great games. Chapter 7 explains techniques for creating games. Sometimes you will see how effortlessly you can convert a simple drill into a great new game. Every game in this book has been widely tested with varied populations. All children will enjoy these games, no matter what their skill level, and you will immediately see their educational value.

How to Teach a Powerful Original Game

To achieve maximum success from each game, follow each of these field-tested ideas and activities before actually playing the games:

- Teach the students how to find personal space and how to move in general space. Having all students move in various directions throughout general space more realistically simulates real-life game situations because most games require players to use multiple pathways. Using a movement approach is extremely helpful in teaching the children to move safely in general space (see the game Far Away, page 161, for an example).

- Most games begin in scatter formation, which is really another name for personal space.

- Spend time discussing safety. Include moving with control, controlling equipment, looking in the direction you are going, avoiding collisions, and staying away from walls and other obstacles.

- Establish clear signals to start and stop movement. Some possible signals to start movement are when the music begins, when you put your hand down, or when you say, "Go." Some signals to stop movement include when the music stops, when you hold your hand up, when you say, "Stop," when you beat a drum, and when you blow a whistle (use a special signal, such as two short whistles). Practice until the students respond quickly.

- Have a clear picture about how a game or activity should progress. If what is physically happening does not conform to your expectations, stop the activity and make adjustments.

- Have a plan to distribute, handle, and collect equipment. Make sure the students know that they must hold equipment still while you are speaking. One technique is to ask the students to sit and place the equipment in their laps, holding it still with both hands. Another is to have them place the equipment on the floor a couple of feet away so that they cannot reach it.

- Ask the students to write their names and class on the top of individual five-by-seven-inch index cards. Keep these cards in class sets. You can use these cards for record keeping. By shuffling the cards, you can quickly and randomly group students and pick student leaders or student monitors.

- Use the maximum amount of equipment available. A piece of equipment for every two to four students is good. A piece of equipment for each student is best. If the students are highly skilled, you may be able to use less equipment. For example, in some of the games you may want to use less equipment and focus more on strategy. The less skilled your students are, the more equipment you should use. Using a maximum amount of equipment gives the students much more practice time and lots more fun. For the more skilled participants, offer more difficult challenges and variations. Even when you do not have students play a game from this book, having them use the maximum amount of equipment drastically cuts down discipline problems, because the students are engaged in play rather than waiting for a turn.

- Many of the games from this book are small-group games. Small-group games offer more activity with less competition and less fear of failure. Use competitive games sparingly and only when students are ready for competition. Competitive games take the focus away from learning (the process) and place it on winning (the product).

- Use developmentally appropriate activities and equipment. If you run a volleyball game for fifth graders using a regulation-size court and a regulation-size volleyball, the game is too hard for many of the students and therefore not developmentally appropriate. The games in this book are developmentally appropriate, and they use developmentally appropriate equipment for all ages and skill levels. The activities are neither too hard nor too easy for the students. Desert Island Volleyball in chapter 5 expands the *Fun, Fitness, and Skills: The Powerful Original Games Approach* format to show how easily the games in this book differentiate instruction.

- Encourage all students to participate by complimenting something they do: "I like the way you helped your partner by throwing the ball carefully." Get to know their names quickly and use them often. Using index cards to call their names will help you remember. Keep moving throughout the play area. Make sure the students are on task. When necessary, survey the whole play area by standing with your back to the wall.

- *Fun, Fitness, and Skills: The Powerful Original Games Approach* will help you to steer clear of many pitfalls in running successful physical education programs. Here are some of the pitfalls to avoid:

  - Giving in to the better athletes' complaints that they want to play kickball or dodgeball. These students need you the least and will take over the game. The quiet ones who really need a good physical education program do not want to play these games.

  - Making yourself a referee or scorekeeper instead of a teacher. If you are calling out a game score as in Steal the Bacon, you are a scorekeeper, not a teacher.

  - Playing games in which most of the students are inactive (although they may appear to be having fun rooting for their teammates). Examples are Steal the Bacon, relay races, elimination games, Duck Duck Goose, line games, and kickball.

  - Allowing the students to choose teams. Use the index cards.

  - Dividing your class in half and playing one team versus the other. This technique will surely focus the attention on the product (winning or losing) rather than the process (learning or improving skills and strategies). Additionally, this kind of activity is sure to create arguments and discipline problems.

  - Employing equipment that can hurt students, such as using a playground ball to play dodgeball.

  - Playing real games with real equipment rather than modifying rules, equipment, court size, and number of players to fit the needs of your students.

- Using drills or having students wait in lines for their turn. Instead, play minigames, use more equipment, and offer challenges that are both cooperative and competitive.

- Allowing the students to hide during a game. In many games students appear to be playing, but in reality they are avoiding the actions the game was designed to include. For example, dodgeball allows students to hide in the back and still stay in the game.

- Giving nonspecific compliments. Saying, "Good job!" is not meaningful because it does not explain what you are referring to. Instead say, "You did a great job of following directions," or "working with many partners," and so on, specifically assessing their performance. Or say, "I really liked the way you responded quickly," or "tried to improve a skill," "helped each other," and so forth.

- Giving prizes for rewards. Rewards are better when they are intrinsic rather than extrinsic. Students know when they are learning and improving. Using a powerful original game accompanied by an encouraging word is far superior to handing out stickers.

CHAPTER 2

Warm-Ups

The typical physical education class begins with warm-ups. For most classes warm-ups consist of some light jogging or jumping, followed by various calisthenic exercises and stretching. If done properly, a good warm-up increases blood flow, stretches and strengthens the muscles, and gets the class ready for work. The problems arise when warm-ups become boring or routinized and classes become difficult to motivate. Teachers are always looking for new and exciting ways to warm up their classes. Choosing a proper warm-up activity often depends on the lesson to follow. For example, when choosing the warm-up game Freedom Fighters (page 8), you can easily adjust the game to the type of lesson that will follow. These warm-up games are great by themselves, and using the additional variations allows for some innovative ways of addressing the ongoing problem of motivation.

Dance Challenge
Ages 7 and up

Topics

- Aerobic endurance
- Locomotor skills
- Cooperation

Objectives

- Psychomotor—Demonstrate various dance steps or locomotor skills.
- Cognitive—Recognize types of dances and understand that dancing is aerobic activity.
- Affective—Cooperate with partners to achieve success.

Equipment

Music

Safety

- Move with control.
- Avoid collisions.

Game

1. Students form a circle without talking to each other. After the students all have a spot in the circle, they take two steps back and maintain the circle.
2. When students hear the music, they must try to follow the leader. You may be the first leader (use a baton or some other implement to designate the leader), or you may pick a student to be the leader. The students attempt to follow the movements of the leader.
3. You may change leaders at any time during the warm-up. Use various kinds of dances. This is a good activity to introduce a new dance step.

Variations

- After they have learned four or five dance steps, students find a partner and choreograph a 1-minute routine using one or more of these dance steps.
- Instead of forming a circle, students begin in their own personal space and perform the dance steps throughout general space.

Everybody's It
Ages 7 and up

Topics

- Aerobic endurance
- Locomotor skills
- Cooperation

Objectives

- Psychomotor—Demonstrate several locomotor skills.
- Cognitive—Understand how to keep the game aerobic.
- Affective—Play honestly and cooperatively.

Equipment

None (or a few small marbles)

Safety

- Move with control.
- Look in the direction you are going.

Game

1. Students spread out in scatter formation.
2. Anyone may tag anyone. When tagged, students freeze until the person who tagged them is tagged. They may then return to the game.
3. Simultaneous tags require both students to freeze for 20 seconds.

Variations

- Allow some children to be decoys. These children may not tag or be tagged. If tagged, they show their identification (such as a beanbag, index card, or marble).
- Change locomotor skills from jogging to skipping to galloping. Allow students to choose their own locomotor skill.

Freedom Fighters
Ages 7 and up

Topics

⊚ Aerobic endurance

⊚ Muscular strength and endurance

⊚ Locomotor skills

⊚ Manipulative skills

Objectives

⊚ Psychomotor—Demonstrate several locomotor skills, balance on various body parts, and manipulate various kinds of equipment.

⊚ Cognitive—Understand the fitness benefits of the game.

⊚ Affective—Show honesty and appreciate individual differences in ability.

Equipment

Various kinds of balls, foam Frisbees, or beanbags

Safety

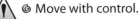

⊚ Move with control.

⊚ Look in the direction you are going.

⊚ Never use a hard piece of equipment.

⊚ Always aim low.

Game

1. Students spread out in scatter formation.

2. Students use the type of equipment you designate. Make this decision based on the lesson to follow. For example, to warm up before a bowling lesson, students can use balls or beanbags so that they can employ proper bowling form to roll the balls or slide the beanbags.

3. Five to seven balls or beanbags of the same type or color are designated as freeze balls or beanbags. Two different colors or types of balls or beanbags are designated as freedom balls or beanbags.

4. The students begin by walking throughout general space. After they begin walking, roll out all of the balls or slide out the beanbags. Once the balls or beanbags are in play, the students may choose a locomotor skill. Do not allow running. Remind students that running is not aerobic and may lead to injury.

5. Any student may pick up any ball or bag. However, after picking up a freeze ball or beanbag, that student may not move until she rolls the ball or slides the beanbag at someone's legs. Students absolutely may not chase someone with the equipment. Students with freedom balls or beanbags may move with the equipment.

6. If a student is hit below the knees by a ball or beanbag, that student freezes with legs apart and arms together above the head. Any student who picks up a freedom ball or beanbag may find a frozen student and roll the ball or slide the beanbag through the frozen student's legs. If this attempt is successful, the frozen student is back in the game. Anyone may pick up the freedom ball or beanbag. If a student is hit below the knee while carrying the freedom ball or beanbag, he must drop it and let someone else pick it up.

7. Students continue the game until the warm-up period is over.

Variations

◉ Vary the kinds of balls. For example, if teaching throwing, use Gator Skin or foam balls. The students must be hit below the waist. Frozen students may catch the freedom ball and become the new freedom fighter. If teaching volleyball, use volleyball trainers or beach balls. Instead of throwing, the students spike the ball at others. Students must always be hit below the waist. Never use a real volleyball or any other hard ball. Freedom fighters may set the ball (overhand pass) to frozen students. Frozen students have to catch the set ball. Of course, you can always change the overhand pass to the forearm pass or serve.

◉ Frozen students balance on various body parts. For example, they freeze in the push-up or crab position and unfreeze if the ball or beanbag goes under their bodies.

◉ Vary the locomotor skills.

Get Set
Ages 4 and up

Topics

◉ Aerobic endurance

◉ Cooperation

◉ Math

Objectives

◉ Psychomotor—Demonstrate several locomotor skills.

◉ Cognitive—Know how to keep the game aerobic; understand the meaning of sets.

◉ Affective—Work cooperatively with all students.

Equipment

Music or none

Safety

 Move with control.

Game

1. Students spread out in scatter formation.
2. Call out a locomotor skill. The students move throughout general space performing that skill.
3. When the music stops, or at a given stop signal, call out a number. The students form a group according to the number called out. Leftover students move to a certain spot on the floor and form a remainder set.

Variations

- Choose various locomotor skills. Have students make shapes according to the number you called. For example, two is a straight line, three is a triangle, and four is a square, rectangle, rhombus, or parallelogram.
- Instruct each group to do a specific exercise together.
- Instruct sets to move together and, upon hearing the stop signal, form new sets based on a mathematical calculation (e.g., three sets of four).

How Many?
Ages 6 and up

Topics

- Aerobic endurance
- Muscular strength and endurance
- Flexibility
- Math
- The FITT principle of exercises: Frequency, Intensity, Time, and Type

Objectives

- Psychomotor—Perform several kinds of exercises using three areas of health-related fitness.
- Cognitive—Understand that the time and type of exercises are important components of fitness.
- Affective—Appreciate differences in ability.

Equipment

None

Safety

 Remind students not to overdo any exercise to the point of exhaustion.

Game

Ask the students, "How many repetitions of a specific exercise can you do in a given amount of time, using correct form?" Using time differentiates instruction and lets students work according to their individual abilities.

Variations

- Vary the amount of time for each exercise.
- Ask the students if they can do a little better each time.

Is It Time Yet?
Ages 5 and up

Topics

- Aerobic endurance
- Math
- The FITT principle of aerobic endurance

Objectives

- Psychomotor—Demonstrate several locomotor skills.
- Cognitive—Have a sense of time; understand that slower movements require more time to achieve the same effect as faster movements.
- Affective—Appreciate differences in ability.

Equipment

Stopwatch

Safety

 Move with control.

Game

1. Students spread out in scatter formation.
2. Students jog for approximately 1 minute. When they think 1 minute is up, students switch to walking.

3. Students continue walking until you tell them to stop.

4. Use a stopwatch and call out, "Stop," after 1 minute. The idea is for the children to try to switch to walking just as or just before you tell them to stop.

Variations

⊚ Change the amount of time to 2 or 3 minutes or change the locomotor skill.

⊚ Choose three children to be the leaders. Each leader chooses a locomotor skill. The students choose one of the leaders to follow.

Partner Ball
Ages 7 and up

Topics

⊚ Aerobic endurance

⊚ Manipulative skills

Objectives

⊚ Psychomotor—Demonstrate various ways of passing a ball while moving.

⊚ Cognitive—Understand the application of force in order to complete a pass.

⊚ Affective—Appreciate differences in ability and cooperate with all partners.

Equipment

1 playground-type ball for every two students

Safety

Make careful passes so as not to hit anyone with the ball.

Game

1. Students start on a line or poly spot.

2. One playground-type ball goes to every two students. Only the person without the ball may move. An odd student may join any pair and make a group of three. In this case, students establish a passing order and keep that order.

3. Students see how many times each pair can go back and forth between their start line and a designated end line by successfully completing passes.

4. Students can try the same activity soccer style. The receiver traps the ball and passes it on.

Variations

⊚ Instruct the students that if they drop a ball, they can try a new skill with the ball. They may later go back to the original skill.

⊚ Vary the kind of equipment. Some examples are footballs, Frisbees, hockey sticks and pucks, basketballs, soccer balls, volleyballs, Nerf balls, Gator Skin balls, and beach balls.

⊚ Require a specific type of pass.

⊚ Require the students to go back to the start line if they drop the ball.

Partner Fitness
Ages 8 and up

Topics

Muscular strength and endurance

Objectives

⊚ Psychomotor—Demonstrate proper push-up position (plank); show proper form for curl-ups.

⊚ Cognitive—Be able to explain how the game increases muscular strength and endurance.

⊚ Affective—Work cooperatively with several partners.

Equipment

1 tennis ball or other small ball for every two students

Safety

Keep touches soft and make sure there are no hard slaps.

Game

1. Partners are close together in scatter formation.

2. Students face their partners in push-up position. While in the push-up position, they alternately touch their partner's right hand three times and the floor twice.

3. After touching hands for the third time, students try to touch one of their partner's hands before the partner touches theirs.

Variations

- ◎ Students place a tennis ball between partners. They proceed as described but try to be the first to grab the tennis ball. They play for a certain amount of time and then switch partners.
- ◎ Students pass a tennis or playground ball between partners while doing fitness exercises such as push-ups or curl-ups.
- ◎ Partners decide which game to play or make up their own fitness game.

Partner Tag
Ages 7 and up

Topics

- ◎ Aerobic endurance
- ◎ Cooperation

Objectives

- ◎ Psychomotor—Demonstrate several locomotor skills.
- ◎ Cognitive—Understand how to keep the game aerobic.
- ◎ Affective—Work cooperatively with various partners.

Equipment

None

Safety

- ◎ Move with control.
- ◎ Look in the direction you are going.

Game

1. Say, "Find a partner by the time I count to 10. Decide who will be It first."
2. One partner spins around once; the other partner walks away (allow only walking).
3. When one partner tags the other, they use the spin-around technique and reverse roles.

Variations

- ◎ Choose a different locomotor skill (do not allow running).
- ◎ After each partner has been tagged once, allow them to become human obstacles. Instead of tagging each other, they walk around providing protection for the students who are not It. Physical blocking is not permitted. After most of the students have become human obstacles, stop the game.

Psychic Warm-Up
Ages 5 and up

Topics

- Aerobic endurance
- Muscular strength and endurance
- Flexibility
- Locomotor skills

Objectives

- Psychomotor—Demonstrate several locomotor skills or several health-related exercises.
- Cognitive—Understand which exercises are related to which areas of fitness.
- Affective—Exhibit honesty and cooperation.

Equipment

None, or 4 traffic cones

Safety

Move with control into the open spaces of the play area.

Game

1. Students begin by sitting close together.
2. Students pick a number between 1 and 25 but do not tell you their numbers.
3. Each student whispers their number to one or two other students (helps prevent cheating).
4. Say, "Try to make me say your number by concentrating all of your psychic powers. Think really hard about your number. Concentrate with all your might. Maintain absolute silence. When I call your number, you may stand and begin jogging around the gymnasium or play area. You can jog either throughout general space or around designated traffic cones." Write the numbers on a piece of paper and cross off each number as it is called.

Variations

- Try some other warm-up exercise in a designated area. Do not allow students to talk. The only sound should be the sound of moving feet.
- After students finish the activity, instruct them to line up in the order they think they were called. See how accurately they line up.

Read and Do
Ages 5 and up

Topics

- Aerobic endurance
- Locomotor skills
- Reading nouns and verbs

Objectives

- Psychomotor—Demonstrate several locomotor skills.
- Cognitive—Read movement verbs and interpret nouns that move; understand why the game is aerobic.
- Affective—Appreciate differences in ability.

Equipment

Large pieces of cardboard or hard paper like oak tag

Safety

- Move with control.
- Look in the direction you are going.

Game

1. Students spread out in scatter formation.
2. Hold up movement words (such as *skip, walk,* and *hop)* written on large pieces of oak tag or cardboard. The students read the words and perform the movements. Nouns like *horse, frog,* and *robot* may also be used.
3. Teach the difference between verbs and nouns. Add adjectives and adverbs by holding up two or three words. For example, hold up phrases like *happy horse, slow frog,* or *sad, fast robot.*

Variations

- Choose three or four children to be It. The Its try to tag the others while performing the appropriate movement. When tagged, students freeze until a new word is held up. Change Its every 1 to 2 minutes.
- Lay all the cards on the floor, faceup. Choose one student to come up and pick a card to hold up. Ask the student to read the card to you before she holds it up. Ask the student whether she picked a noun or a verb. Pick a new student to come up after every 30 seconds of movement.

Reading Exchange
Ages 6 and up

Topics

- Aerobic endurance
- Locomotor skills
- Social skills
- Reading nouns and verbs

Objectives

- Psychomotor—Demonstrate several locomotor skills.
- Cognitive—Read movement verbs and interpret nouns that move; understand why the game is aerobic.
- Affective—Exhibit honesty and appreciate differences in reading ability.

Equipment

Index cards with words written on them

Safety

- Move with control.
- Look in the direction you are going.

Game

1. Students spread out in scatter formation.
2. Each person has an index card with a movement verb or noun written on it.
3. The students move through general space as their card tells them or interpret the way the noun would move.
4. At a given signal, students exchange cards with someone else.

Variation

Give the cards to only half the students. The other half attempts to tag someone with a card. They must be moving the same way as the person they tag. They then try to guess what the card says. If the student guesses right, they exchange jobs.

There, Their, and They're
Ages 8 and up

Topics

⊚ Aerobic endurance

⊚ Locomotor skills

⊚ Understanding homophones

Objectives

⊚ Psychomotor—Demonstrate several locomotor skills.

⊚ Cognitive—Understand the meaning of homophones; explain why the game is aerobic.

⊚ Affective—Appreciate differences in ability to understand homophones.

Equipment

Large pieces of cardboard

Safety

⚠ Move carefully from line to line so that no one trips over anyone else's legs.

Game

1. Students spread out in scatter formation.

2. Large words on cardboard are placed on four walls as follows: *there* and *there* on opposite walls, and *their* and *they're* on opposite walls.

3. Read sentences that contain one of these words. Upon hearing the complete sentence (for example, "They're coming home after school"), the students jog, skip, or gallop to the black, or taped, line in front of the wall with the proper word.

Variations

⊚ Use more than one word ("They went over there to pick up their books"). In this case, the students remember the order and go to more than one black, or taped, line.

⊚ Four students hold up the different signs. Each of these students performs a locomotor skill. The class copies the student who is holding up the correct homophone. This variation works well when there are no available lines.

⊚ Use other homophones.

⊚ Use gym scooters. When students use scooters, the game's focus changes from aerobic endurance to muscular strength and endurance.

CHAPTER 3

Fitness Games

The games in this chapter promote the three main areas of health-related physical fitness: aerobic endurance, muscular strength and endurance, and flexibility. Many of the games also include fundamental sport-related skills and skill-related fitness. Introduce each game by discussing the fitness components of the game. During the game's explanation and demonstration, point out how to achieve the game's maximum fitness benefit. After each game, let the students explain how this game helped their fitness. You may also modify many of the fitness games to use as warm-up activities.

April Fools' Hunt
Ages 6 and up

This game was created for April 1. Of course students can play it on any day; they simply don't say the words *April fool*. The game is based on the simple concept of hiding and finding, a favorite age-old children's activity.

Topics

- Aerobic endurance
- Muscular strength and endurance
- Locomotor skills
- Teamwork

Objectives

- Psychomotor—Demonstrate several locomotor skills or show various ways to manipulate a gym scooter.
- Cognitive—Understand the fitness benefits of the game.
- Affective—Show teamwork in order to achieve success.

Equipment

- 1 gym scooter for each participant (or no scooters, as in the first variation)
- 40 to 60 traffic cones, dome markers, or poly spots
- 40 pennies or plastic eggs
- A bag to hold the pennies or eggs

Safety

Review safety rules for scooters. If students are not using scooters, remind them to move with control and look in the direction they are going.

Game

1. Each student receives 2 or 3 traffic cones, dome markers, or poly spots. If they are using pennies, poly spots work the best.
2. The students place these items randomly throughout the play area.
3. Each student gets a scooter.
4. One child is the leader. The leader goes to a central location outside the play area. There is a new leader for each round.

5. About one-fifth of the class comes to the front. These students are the hiders.

6. The hiders divide the pennies among themselves. They sit on their scooters and hide pennies under the poly spots. They may place one or more pennies under each spot. Some spots may not have any pennies placed under them. They may also keep two pennies, one in each hand. Small plastic eggs may substitute for the pennies. In this case, use traffic cones or dome markers instead of poly spots.

7. Students begin the game in scatter formation.

8. The rest of the students lie on their bellies on the scooters. They are the seekers. On the go signal, the seekers attempt to find the pennies. They may find only one at a time. If they pick up a traffic cone or poly spot and see more than one penny, they may take only one. They immediately bring the penny back to the leader, who places it in the bag and counts the pennies as they come in. After bringing the penny to the leader, the seeker may go back and look for more.

9. The seekers may also tag any hider. Upon being tagged, the hider opens his hands. If he has a penny, he gives it to the seeker. If not, he just says, "April fool!"

10. At any time during the game, the hiders may also choose to pass the pennies to each other or to change locations of pennies from one poly spot to another.

11. When students have found all the pennies, stop the game and choose a different group to hide the pennies.

Variations

◉ Instead of using scooters, the students perform a variety of locomotor skills. For example, the hiders jog or skip, and the seekers gallop or walk. Note that this variation makes the game more aerobic but takes away from muscular endurance. You should discuss this fitness factor with them.

◉ The hiders wear pinnies as identification.

◉ Play this game as hide-and-seek on any day.

◉ Divide the class into small teams of five or six players. Give each team a chance to hide the pennies. Divide the game into time segments so that each team has an equal amount of time to hide and try to keep the pennies. The team that holds on to the most pennies or keeps the pennies longest is the winner.

Ball Exchange
Ages 8 and up

This game combines aerobic fitness with passing and catching practice. Encourage the students to keep moving. Explain that in most games that use balls, successful players know how to move without the ball and how to catch a ball while moving.

Topics

- Aerobic endurance
- Locomotor skills
- Manipulative skills
- Cooperation

Objectives

- Psychomotor—Demonstrate several locomotor skills while tossing and catching a ball.
- Cognitive— Judge the speed at which to move in order to keep the game aerobic; judge the application of force applied to a ball in order to make successful ball exchanges.
- Affective—Cooperate to keep the game moving while working to achieve a group goal.

Equipment

Various kinds of balls, 1 for each participant

Safety

- Move with control.
- Watch for other groups.

Game

1. The object of the game is to complete as many successful passes as possible within a given amount of time. Each time period lasts between 2 and 5 minutes, depending on the age and fitness level of the class. A successful pass is defined as a ball that is caught on the fly.
2. The entire class or group works together. All caught passes are totaled at the end of the set time period. The students are responsible for keeping track of their own catches.

3. Students use as many kinds of balls as possible.

4. Students begin the game in scatter formation, evenly spread out over the play area.

5. At the start signal, the students choose a locomotor skill and begin moving throughout the play area. The students can change the kind of locomotor skill they are performing at any time.

6. Students choose from the following skills: jogging, skipping, galloping, hopping, and sliding.

7. While performing the chosen locomotor skill, each student attempts to toss the ball to another student; at the same time, the chosen receiver tosses her own ball to the student who threw to her. Students make eye contact or communicate verbally with the chosen receiver to accomplish this simultaneous exchange.

8. At the stop signal, each student reports the number of successful catches.

9. Students begin again and try to beat the previous score.

Variations

⚙ Take the final count and multiply it by another number. If a student answers the multiplication example correctly within 10 seconds, the class scores a bonus of five catches.

⚙ Count only passes and catches that are caught by both tossers.

⚙ Use only one kind of ball.

⚙ Allow only one kind of toss or throw.

⚙ Give a ball to only half the class. Passes are made with a single ball at a time.

⚙ Allow the ball to bounce one or more times.

⚙ Each student counts his catches and attempts to beat his score in each new round.

⚙ Choose two or more students to be distracters.

　　⚙ The distracters' job is to try to intercept passes. These students do not start the game with a ball. When a distracter intercepts a pass, she gets one point. The distracters keep their own point totals. The intercepting distracter returns the ball to the person who tossed it.

　　⚙ If a student's ball is intercepted twice, he goes outside the court and tosses the ball to himself 10 times before reentering the game. The student may also toss the ball against the wall (or to another student who is outside the court) or may choose another kind of ball.

Bowlers and Setters
Ages 7 and up

This is a wonderful aerobic activity that also includes target practice. Dividing the students into pairs ensures almost constant movement with very little waiting.

Topics

- Aerobic endurance
- Manipulative skills
- Cooperation
- Teamwork

Objectives

- Psychomotor—Move continuously for 2 to 3 minutes; slide beanbags accurately from varying distances.
- Cognitive—Understand the aerobic benefits of the game; understand the application of force necessary to slide a beanbag accurately.
- Affective—Cooperate to keep the game moving and safe.

Equipment

- 1 or 2 beanbags for each pair of students
- 10 to 20 plastic bowling pins or tennis ball cans

Safety

- Make sure to slide beanbags, not throw them.
- Joggers should always jog on the outside of the play area and in the same direction.

Game

1. Students divide into pairs. An extra student may be in one group of three. This group should begin the game with two bowlers and one setter. Both bowlers begin with two beanbags.
2. Each pair of students receives two beanbags. One student in each pair begins the game as the bowler (with the beanbags); the other student begins the game as the setter.
3. Place the bowlers at a starting line (e.g., at one end of a basketball court). The bowlers spread out along the width of the starting line (see figure 3.1).
4. Set the bowling pins on the other side of the play area, about midway between the opposite end line and the centerline. The pins should be

evenly spread out in a straight line across the width of the play area. The distance of the pins from the centerline may vary, depending on the age and ability of the class.

5. The setters begin the game at the opposite end from the bowlers and behind the pins.

6. On the go signal, all the bowlers move forward as far as they like, but not past the centerline. They slide the two beanbags one at a time, using a bowling motion, and attempt to knock down any pin or pins.

7. After sliding the beanbags, the bowler returns to the starting line to wait for a setter to bring her two beanbags. As soon as the bowler is handed the beanbags, she may bowl them and return to the line.

8. The setters each pick up two beanbags and jog on the outside of the basketball lines in a counterclockwise direction. They hand the beanbags to the first bowler in line. They then continue to jog on the outside of the play area, back behind the pins, to retrieve more beanbags.

9. After about 2 minutes, students count how many pins were knocked down. The setters reset the pins and exchange jobs with the bowlers.

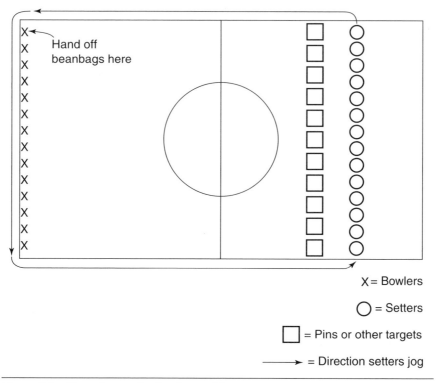

X = Bowlers

O = Setters

☐ = Pins or other targets

⟶ = Direction setters jog

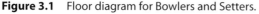

Figure 3.1   Floor diagram for Bowlers and Setters.

Variations

- Time how long it takes to knock down all the pins. Try to beat the best time.
    - Cooperative—The whole class works together.
    - Competitive—Each pair or group of three keeps track of its own score.
- Set each pin at a different distance from the centerline.
- Use a scatter formation. Choose half the class to knock down the pins. Give each of these students one beanbag. The remaining students, except for three, choose one pin each and attempt to protect the pin by blocking the sliding beanbags with hands or feet. The leftover three students set the fallen pins back up. See how many pins are down after each 2-minute round. Exchange jobs. The students trying to knock down the pins have to actually release the beanbags from their hands. After each attempt, the bowler may pick up one beanbag that is loose on the floor and move on to a different target. This variation is less aerobic; you should discuss the reasons with the class.

Cardio Obstacle Course
Ages 8 and up

This obstacle course allows you to be creative by varying the kind of equipment used. The advantage of this game is in the setup. Students monitor themselves. You are free to move around, giving advice and help where needed. Discuss the word *cardio* as it relates to aerobic endurance.

Topics

- Aerobic endurance
- Muscular strength and endurance
- Locomotor skills
- Manipulative skills
- Leadership skills
- Cooperation

Objectives

- Psychomotor—Demonstrate at least two categories of physical fitness, including aerobic endurance.
- Cognitive—Judge the speed at which to work in order to keep the course aerobic.

⊚ Affective—Appreciate individual differences in ability; work cooperatively to keep the activities moving.

Equipment

Use as much equipment as possible to keep the obstacle course exciting. The following are some examples of equipment:

⊚ Traffic cones

⊚ Long and short jump ropes

⊚ Hula hoops

⊚ Mats

⊚ Various kinds of balls

⊚ Foam dice

⊚ Pull-up bar

⊚ Pegboard

⊚ Rock wall

⊚ Climbing rope

⊚ Gym scooters

⊚ Crates or boxes to use as targets

Safety

Make sure the students know how to use each piece of equipment.

Game

1. Each student has a partner. An odd student goes into one group of three. Each pair of students works together. One partner performs the obstacle course while the other partner acts as a guide or helper. If there is one group of three, two students perform the obstacle course. The helper's job is to guide the partner through the course, reset obstacles, retrieve equipment, and so forth. Both partners work at a moderate pace. At the end of the course, they switch jobs.

2. The objective is to go through the course as many times as possible in the time allowed, working at a moderate pace. Students learn to monitor their own pulses; they may use heart rate monitors if available.

3. Some possible activities include (but are not limited to) curl-ups; push-ups; going under, over, or around objects; swinging on a climbing rope onto a mat; jumping rope; shooting a basketball or soccer ball; balancing an object on a body part or on a piece of equipment; riding on a gym scooter; performing a gymnastic move; doing a pull-up or chin-up; climbing a pegboard or simply hanging by the pegs for a count of five; pushing or pulling an object; and traversing a rock wall.

4. Explain to the students that they are not racing each other. They are working at a moderate pace to increase their own individual fitness.

5. To keep the waiting at a minimum, the students begin at various points along the course but continue in the same direction, generally either clockwise or counterclockwise, around the play area. Obstacles may be numbered also.

6. Students may skip or modify a part of the course that they find too difficult.

Variations

⊚ Rather than working in pairs, the class divides into groups. One group becomes the supervisors. Since one supervisor is needed for each obstacle, the number of students in each group depends on the number of obstacles. For example, if there are eight obstacles, divide the class into groups of eight. The supervisors make sure the obstacles are used correctly. They also reset them when necessary. Rotate each group so that they all have a chance to supervise and a chance to perform the obstacle course. The students performing the obstacle course should know which group they belong to, but they perform the course individually. All students, except for the supervisors, perform the obstacle course at the same time.

⊚ Allocate points to each area of the obstacle course according to difficulty. Students keep track of their own points (they may use a log or fitness diary). A student gains points only by completing a part of the course successfully. In this game it is best to have the supervisors judge the points. You can post signs and directions at each obstacle.

Collection
Ages 8 and up

The students practice eye–hand coordination by tossing and catching balls while on the move.

Topics

⊚ Aerobic endurance

⊚ Locomotor skills

⊚ Manipulative skills

⊚ Cooperation

Objectives

- Psychomotor—Demonstrate tossing and catching skills while performing locomotor skills.
- Cognitive—Understand the game's aerobic benefits.
- Affective—Appreciate individual differences in ability and cooperate to keep the game safe.

Equipment

- 1 soft-type ball for each student
- 1 bucket or bag
- 1 stopwatch

Safety

- The balls should be released high enough to come down in a fairly straight arc.
- When tennis balls are used, instruct the students to look up not as the balls are released but after they have bounced.
- If students play the game indoors or in a small area, use soft balls like Nerf, foam, or fleece.

Game

1. A bucket or bag is in a designated area.
2. Each student receives a ball.
3. Students spread out in scatter formation.
4. At the start signal, students move throughout the play area while tossing and catching their balls. You time the round.
5. Students practice this skill until the majority can move while simultaneously tossing and catching the ball.
6. When you give a signal (whistle, stopping of music, drumbeat), the students toss the balls backward over their heads in a high arc.
7. Students pick up as many balls as they can possibly carry and return them to the bucket or bag, using only the arms and hands. They may not use clothing to carry the balls.
8. The round continues until students have picked up all the balls and you note the end time.
9. Students redistribute the balls and begin another round.
10. The class sees whether it can beat its best time.

Variations

- ◎ Vary the locomotor skills.
- ◎ Vary the ways the students toss and catch the balls. For example, they toss with one hand and catch with two, toss with the right hand and catch with the left, and so forth.
- ◎ Cooperative—Designate one-sixth of the students as ball carriers. The other students try to pick up the balls and hand them to the ball carriers. The ball carriers must be able to hold the balls in their arms. Time the students to see how quickly they can gather the balls. Next time see whether they can beat their record. You may also set a time limit; for example, see how many balls students can pick up in 20 seconds.
- ◎ Competitive—Divide the class into equal teams of five or six players. One student on each team is the designated ball carrier. The carrier may not use clothing to hold the balls. See how many balls each carrier is holding when all the balls are picked up.

Concentration
Ages 7 and up

Remember Concentration, the memory card game? This version requires humans to move. When students use equipment, they obtain the added benefit of practicing eye–hand or eye–foot coordination.

Topics

- ◎ Aerobic endurance
- ◎ Locomotor skills
- ◎ Manipulative skills

Objectives

- ◎ Psychomotor—Demonstrate several locomotor skills or perform various manipulative skills while moving throughout the play area.
- ◎ Cognitive—Understand the need to concentrate in order to memorize; understand that movement increases heart rate.
- ◎ Affective—Move cooperatively in general space.

Equipment

The equipment may be the same kind for each student, or students may choose from a variety of equipment that they can manipulate:

◎ None, or 1 piece of equipment for each student, such as the following:
  ◎ Various kinds of balls
  ◎ Beanbags
  ◎ Scarves
  ◎ Hoops

Safety

Remind students to move with control and watch where they are going.

Game

1. The students find personal space and are instructed to memorize this approximate spot in the play area.
2. Students practice moving away from and returning to this spot.
3. One student comes to the front and attempts to memorize everyone's spot.
4. This student observes for about 30 seconds. The observation time may vary depending on the developmental ability of the students.
5. Name a locomotor skill. The students manipulate their equipment while moving throughout general space.
6. After 1 to 2 minutes, stop the students' movement and call out the names of two students.
7. The student who has been observing attempts to escort these two students back to their original personal spots.
8. The observer then chooses someone else to take his place.
9. After each round, all the students go back to their original spots so that the new student in the front can try to memorize all their locations.

Variations

◎ Students choose from a variety of locomotor skills.
◎ Students choose from a variety of equipment.
◎ Allow students to use each piece of equipment only one way, or let them choose from a variety of ways.
◎ Ask the students to exchange their equipment with each other after a given time.

Cooperative Catch
Ages 8 and up

Here is an aerobic game that fosters teamwork, cooperation, strategy, and tossing and catching skills.

Topics

- Aerobic endurance
- Locomotor skills
- Manipulative skills
- Cooperation

Objectives

- Psychomotor—Be able to jog while tossing and catching a ball at least three consecutive times.
- Cognitive—Understand and explain the aerobic benefits of the game; understand the application of force necessary for tossing and catching a ball while moving.
- Affective—Cooperate to achieve success; accept and appreciate individual differences in ability.

Equipment

- 1 playground or soft-type ball for every three to five students
- 1 stopwatch

Safety

The groups should seek to move into the open spaces and avoid other groups as they move.

Game

1. Divide the class into groups of three to five students.
2. Distribute one playground, foam, fleece, or other type of soft ball to each group.
3. Students spread out in scatter formation, with group members standing close together.

4. Give each group a minute to establish an order of tossing and catching so that each group member gets an equal chance.

5. Instruct the groups to jog continuously during the game. Each group jogs throughout the play area while continuously tossing the ball to each other.

6. The group counts the number of successful consecutive catches. If the ball lands on the floor, the group begins the count again, attempting to beat its previous record.

7. Time each round for 2 to 3 minutes.

Variations

⑥ Vary the locomotor skill.

⑥ Assign a minimum height to which students must toss the ball; for example, they must toss the ball above the head.

⑥ Specify that the ball may be caught on one, two, or three bounces.

⑥ Play any lively music. When the music stops, the student with the ball moves to a new group.

⑥ When a group member drops the ball, the group must jog around the ball until a student from another group picks it up and gives it to them. Since this act of kindness may result in a lower catch total, the helping group may add five bonus catches for each group they help.

⑥ Each group decides on the type of tosses it wishes to make and on a goal number of consecutive catches. When members meet their goal, they report their score to you or the leader. Then instruct them to practice until the round is over. Each round should last at least 3 minutes, but at your discretion it may last as long as 5 minutes. After the round is completed, do one or more of the following:

   ⑥ Match two or more groups who achieved approximately the same goal. These groups compete against each other in the next round.

   ⑥ Exchange one or two players from one group for one or two players in another group. See whether the groups can still reach or improve on their previous goals.

   ⑥ After a set number of consecutive catches, the group exchanges its ball for another kind. They report the effect of the new ball on the score.

Crossfire
Ages 8 and up

Here is a new and exciting version of Running Bases. Don't worry too much about the students' catching and throwing abilities. The idea is to move as much as possible with very little rest.

Topics

- Aerobic endurance
- Manipulative skills
- Cooperation
- Teamwork

Objectives

- Psychomotor—Be able to move continuously for 5 to 10 minutes while changing directions quickly; be able to throw and catch a ball from varying distances.
- Cognitive—Understand the nature of aerobic endurance; use strategy to achieve success; understand the principles of force and absorption.
- Affective—Appreciate individual differences in ability; cooperate to keep the game moving and safe.

Equipment

- 5 bases marked off with lines, floor tape, or poly spots
- 4 Gator Skin or heavy foam-type balls

Safety

⚠ Move with control and avoid collisions.

Game

1. Mark off bases in the four corners of the play area. The bases should be large enough to accommodate at least five players. Mark off a larger base in the center of the play area.
2. Choose eight students to become the initial catchers. The catchers stand in front of the base area. Each corner catcher faces a center catcher. Give one ball to each corner catcher to begin the game. The corner and her center catcher throw the ball back and forth to each other. When a runner (or runners) decides to try to go from corner to center or center to corner, the catchers attempt to tag the runners with the ball (see figure 3.2).

3. Divide the rest of the class equally among the four base areas in the corners.

4. The object of the game is to go to all four corners without being tagged by a catcher. The catcher must tag the runner with the ball. Each runner must go from his starting corner to the center base and then back to a different corner, always alternating between a corner and the center. If tagged, the runner must go back to his original base and start over.

5. When a runner makes it successfully to all four corners, he reports to you or the leader. Give a number from one to eight to the students as they report. The first eight students become the next catchers. However, after reporting to you or the leader, the student should start over and continue playing until the round is over.

6. How long to make each round is at your discretion. If everyone is to have a chance to become a catcher, the class divides into groups of eight. Give each group a number. When you call that number, those eight players become the catchers. If you have four groups of eight, divide the playing time by four so that all groups have a chance to catch.

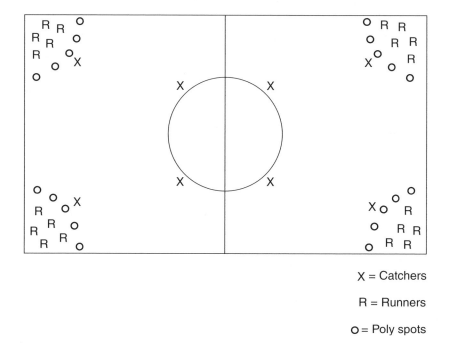

X = Catchers

R = Runners

o = Poly spots

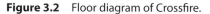

Figure 3.2   Floor diagram of Crossfire.

Variations

- To make the game more aerobic, the students receive one point for each new base reached. If tagged, they go back to the previous base.
- Allow the students to go from corner to corner as well as from corner to center. Students may move randomly to any base. Count one point for each base successfully reached.
- To make the game more aerobic, each runner must move continuously. She cannot stop at any base for more than a three-count. The catchers count to three. At three, they may tag the runner even if she is still on the base. If tagged, the runner goes back to her previous base and deducts one point.
- As in Running Bases, each student gets three outs. He can accumulate points in any of the above ways until the third out. After the third out, he goes back to zero and begins again, trying to better the previous score.
- Divide the class into teams of eight players.
  - Extra students may become extra runners. If there is an extra student on the catching team, she becomes the leader for the round. Players report all scores to her.
  - After a set amount of time, the teams report their points.
  - Change the catching team.
  - The catching team that allows the fewest points is the winner. Alternatively, the individual team scoring the most points is the winner. Or both teams may be declared the winners. Points may be obtained by any of the above methods.

Egg Soccer
Ages 8 and up

The more Wiffle balls in play, the more fun. The game was originally created to coincide with Easter, but of course it can be played anytime, with or without the eggs.

Topics

- Aerobic endurance
- Manipulative skills
- Cooperation
- Safety awareness

Objectives

- Psychomotor—Manipulate a ball with the feet; move continuously for 3-minute periods.
- Cognitive—Be able to explain the fitness benefits of the game; develop an effective strategy.
- Affective—Move safely; appreciate individual differences in ability; exhibit honest behavior.

Equipment

- 30 or more plastic eggs
- 4 to 6 tennis cans with covers, to hold the eggs
- 20 to 30 poly spots
- 30 to 50 Wiffle balls

Safety

Be careful not to trip on all the rolling balls.

Game

1. Students divide into groups of four or five.
2. One group begins the game as the egg goalies. They spread out in the four corners of the play area. If there are five players, one player can find space at the midpoint of the play area near the sideline.
3. Each egg goalie gets five poly spots and one tennis can filled with half-eggs.
4. The goalie places the tennis can in the center of his area. The poly spots are placed around the tennis can, forming a restricted area. Each restricted area should be about 8 to 10 square feet (0.7 to 0.9 square meters).
5. Everyone else is in scatter formation throughout the play area.
6. Students are reminded to move carefully so as not to trip on rolling Wiffle balls.
7. The Wiffle balls are dumped out to begin the game.
8. The students try to dribble and kick the Wiffle balls so that they knock down the tennis can. The goalie may protect the can with the feet but not the hands. The goalie may not make contact with the tennis can while trying to protect it. The goalie stays in the restricted area. The other players may not enter the restricted area.

9. A player who successfully knocks down a tennis can enters the restricted area, opens the can, takes a half-egg, closes the can, and resets it. The player then deposits the half-egg in a designated egg area (a box or hula hoop in the center of the play area) and reenters the game.

10. Students play for 3 minutes and then count the half-eggs.

11. Play a new round with another group of goalies.

12. The team that gives up the fewest half-eggs may be declared the winner.

Variations

◎ Instead of using eggs, place pennies or puzzle pieces in the can.

◎ Play the same game without goalies or teams. When a student knocks down the can, she collects one object from the can, resets the can, and continues to play. She must hold the objects in one or both hands. The student holding the most objects at the end of the round is the winner.

  ◎ Cooperative—After the designated time is up, students total the number of objects removed from the cans and then try to beat this score next round.

  ◎ Individual—Students try to beat their previous scores.

Figure It Out
Ages 4 and up

This game is based on the old game called Indian Chief. Make up your own name or just call it Figure It Out. Whatever you choose to call it, the students will have fun while gaining aerobic fitness and eye–hand or eye–foot coordination skills.

Topics

◎ Aerobic endurance

◎ Locomotor skills

◎ Manipulative skills

◎ Leadership and followership skills

Objectives

◎ Psychomotor—Be able to perform at least five locomotor skills (ages 4 to 7). Combine at least five locomotor skills with hand dribbling or tossing and catching a ball (ages 8 and up).

◎ Cognitive—Recognize ways to move and see the relationship between movement and heart rate (ages 4 to 7). Understand the aerobic benefits of the game (ages 8 and up).

◎ Affective—Be able to follow simple rules to make a game successful.

Equipment

◎ None for ages 4 to 7

◎ 1 playground ball or other kind of manipulative for each student ages 8 and up

Safety

⚠ Move with control and watch where you are going.

Game

1. Each student (ages 8 and up) receives a piece of equipment.

2. Choose one student to come to the front of the play area and hide his eyes. Once the game starts, it will be this student's job to guess which student is the leader.

3. All other students are in scatter formation.

4. Choose another student to be the leader. Do not call this student by name, but walk over and have the student raise her hand high in the air.

5. The leader begins a locomotor skill. The rest of the students perform the same skill as the leader. Ages 8 and up perform a manipulative skill with their equipment as well. Students do not follow directly behind the leader but watch the leader out of the corners of their eyes and move in various pathways throughout general space. They may practice with several leaders before actually playing the game; this is a good time to discuss peripheral vision, which is so necessary for almost any sport as well as for many life skills.

6. Once movement has started, the student who has been hiding his eyes turns around and observes the action. The rest of the game can be played in one of two ways:

   ◎ The leader changes the locomotor skill at any time. Everyone else changes to the leader's movement as quickly as possible. The student who is guessing may stop the action at any time and try to guess who the leader is. Give this student three guesses.

   ◎ Call out, "Change!" At that time the leader must change the locomotor skill. Tell students to change three times and then give the guessing student one guess.

   ◎ In either case, after the guesser attempts to pick the leader, that guesser may pick the next person to hide eyes and guess.

Variations

- Change the name of the game to Moving President, CEO, Find the Groundhog, Who's the Boss, or some such title.
- Require the leader to perform skills for a specific sport.
- Choose more than one leader and allow students to follow any of the leaders.
- Allow the students ages 8 and up to change the way they are manipulating the equipment, the locomotor skill, or both.

Fitness Ball
Ages 7 and up

Empty your closet of balls and promote cooperation and sharing with aerobic fitness and manipulative skills. The students have fun using all the various kinds of balls while maintaining almost constant motion.

Topics

- Aerobic endurance
- Manipulative skills
- Cooperation
- Safety awareness

Objectives

- Psychomotor—Perform at least three locomotor skills while manipulating various kinds of balls.
- Cognitive—Understand the game's aerobic nature; understand the application of force necessary for controlling a ball.
- Affective—Cooperate to exchange equipment quickly; move safely into the open areas.

Equipment

1 ball of any kind for each student (soccer balls, basketballs, playground balls, Gator Skin balls, Nerf balls, and so on)

Safety

 Move with control and watch where you are going.

Game

1. Each student receives one ball.

2. Students spread out in scatter formation.

3. Remind students to be aware of others so that there will be no collisions.

4. On the go signal, the students choose a locomotor skill. They perform this skill while manipulating their balls.

5. On a given signal, they exchange equipment with another student. The objective is to get a new piece of equipment each time. If they get the same kind of ball, they attempt a different locomotor skill or a different way of manipulating the ball.

6. Students get a brief rest period every 3 to 5 minutes. During this time, choose a few students to demonstrate how they were manipulating the balls.

Variations

- Students score one point for each new piece of equipment.
- Students score one point for performing each locomotor skill.
- Students work with partners; they share equipment or play Follow the Leader.
- Students play tag—anyone may tag anyone else. If tagged, students exchange balls. This variation is for more advanced players. Taggers must be performing a skill with their equipment when tagging.

Fitness Exchange
Ages 8 and up

Want to combine manipulative skills with fitness awareness assessment? Here is the perfect game. You will immediately be able to recognize which students understand the fitness categories. The students will also receive practice in eye–hand or eye–foot coordination.

Topics

- Aerobic endurance
- Muscular strength and endurance
- Flexibility
- Locomotor skills
- Manipulative skills

Objectives

- ⊚ Psychomotor—Demonstrate a variety of locomotor skills while manipulating a ball; perform exercises that demonstrate aerobic conditioning, muscular strength and endurance, and flexibility.
- ⊚ Cognitive—Understand which kinds of exercises are used for each category of fitness.
- ⊚ Affective—Enjoy activities that promote fitness.

Equipment

1 ball of any type, or any other manipulative, for each student

Safety

Move with control and watch where you are going.

Game

1. Distribute one piece of equipment to each student.
2. Students spread out in scatter formation.
3. At the start signal, the students perform a locomotor or manipulative skill with their equipment. For example, they can toss and catch a ball, jump back and forth over a rope, self-set and bump a volleyball, or dribble a playground ball with hands or feet throughout the play area.
4. At the stop signal (whistle, music stopping, musical instrument), the students stop and listen for a fitness category.
5. Call out one of the following categories: aerobic, flexibility, upper-body strength and endurance, abdominal strength and endurance, and so forth.
6. The students demonstrate an exercise (with or without their equipment) that corresponds to the stated category.
7. After 1 or 2 minutes, students begin a new manipulative or locomotor activity.

Variations

- ⊚ Distribute more than one piece of equipment to each student.
- ⊚ Give each student the same kind of equipment.
- ⊚ Give more advanced students more specific categories to demonstrate. For example, ask them to demonstrate an exercise that increases quadriceps flexibility.
- ⊚ Ask the students to work in groups, with one or more pieces of equipment for each group.
- ⊚ Ask the students to demonstrate the exercises with a partner.

Fitness Feud
Ages 5 and up

This game is based on the old television game show *Family Feud*. This simple twist on aerobic fitness, movement, and manipulative skills spices up practice. Fitness Feud also adds easy assessment of the students' knowledge of levels and sport skills.

Topics

- Aerobic endurance
- Locomotor skills
- Manipulative skills

Objectives

- Psychomotor—Demonstrate several locomotor skills and three levels (ages 5 to 7). Perform assorted manipulative skills while moving throughout the play area (ages 8 and up).
- Cognitive—Recognize locomotor skills and levels and understand that movement increases heart rate (ages 5 to 7). Understand mature motor patterns for manipulating equipment and understand the game's aerobic benefits (ages 8 and up).
- Affective—Appreciate individual differences in ability.

Equipment

- None for ages 5 to 7
- 1 piece of equipment for each student ages 8 and up. For example, you can use any of the following:
  - Tennis balls
  - Basketballs
  - Soccer balls
  - Volleyballs
  - Scarves
  - Beanbags
  - Hoops

Safety

Move with control and watch where you are going.

Game

1. Students spread out in scatter formation.

2. Two students are chosen to come and stand next to you or the leader.

3. Students begin a locomotor skill according to your or the leader's directions: "Skip throughout the play area without touching anyone or anything. When I say to stop, freeze at a high, medium, or low level."

4. The two students observing the action take turns whispering to you at what level they think the greatest number of students will freeze. The student with the correct answer scores one point. If both students choose the same answer, give them another chance with a new question.

5. After the observers have two tries, two new students come up.

6. Here is an example of a challenge that uses a piece of equipment: "Can you jog throughout the play area while tossing and catching a tennis ball and then, when I give the stop signal, can you show me either the correct overhand throwing motion or the correct two-handed catching motion?" The selected students decide before each challenge how they think the greatest number of players will freeze. For instance, in the preceding example they decide whether the greatest number will show the throwing motion or the catching motion. Another example is to have students dribble a basketball; on the stop signal, they hold the ball as they would for an overhead pass, a chest pass, or a football pass.

Variation

When the two students come up, ask them to place their hands on their heads and face each other. Extend one hand with palm up between the two students. Ask a question dealing with physical fitness or general knowledge. The first student to touch your hand answers the question. If that student gives a correct answer and also accurately determines how the greatest number of players will freeze, she receives two points: one point for answering the question and one point for determining how the majority of the players will freeze. If she gives an incorrect answer, the other student may receive one point if he determines correctly how the majority of the players will freeze.

Fitness Island
Ages 5 and up

Sometimes children like to use their imaginations. On this pretend island, they get to do many fun fitness activities. Use the directions provided, but feel free to add your own. For ages 5 to 7, modify the game by using fewer directions, keeping them simple, and practicing each direction more times before playing the game.

Topics

- ⑥ Aerobic endurance
- ⑥ Muscular strength and endurance
- ⑥ Locomotor skills
- ⑥ Cooperation
- ⑥ Listening skills
- ⑥ Geographical concepts
- ⑥ Safety awareness

Objectives

- ⑥ Psychomotor—Perform various exercises and locomotor skills.
- ⑥ Cognitive—Recognize the geographical directions north, south, east, and west; remember the proper response to several verbal cues; understand the game's fitness benefits; learn to monitor their pulse.
- ⑥ Affective—Enjoy activities that promote fitness; move safely as a group from place to place; work cooperatively to achieve success.

Equipment

None, or 1 gym scooter for each student

Safety

- ⑥ Move carefully in general space; be careful not to bump into other moving students.
- ⑥ Review the safety rules for gym scooters (if used).

Game

1. The play area is an island.
2. The outside lines of the basketball court are the island's perimeter. If there are no lines available, poly spots or traffic cones can make up perimeter lines.
3. You are the island's leader, and the students respond by moving as quickly as possible to the proper location.
4. Students spread out in scatter formation.
5. Introduce the commands a few at a time and run some practice rounds. When the students are comfortable with the instructions, take them through a prearranged sequence of commands. They can then repeat the same sequence for each round.
6. Time how long it takes the students to complete each round and challenges them to attempt to beat their own world record.

Commands for Fitness Island

- Directions—For directions north, south, east, west, and equator (center), ask the students to power walk. Power walking is a safe method of movement when everyone is moving in the same direction. However, feel free to try other locomotor skills.

  - North—Students power walk to a line near the north side of the play area.
  - South—Students power walk to a line near the south side of the play area.
  - East—Students power walk to a line near the east side of the play area.
  - West—Students power walk to a line near the west side of the play area.
  - Equator—The equator is the center circle of the play area. Students straddle jump the centerline.

- School—Students quickly sit and pretend they are writing a composition.
- Farmer—Everyone quickly finds a partner. The pairs work together forming a wheelbarrow, with one partner holding the ankles of the other and walking. Call out to reverse, and students change places.
- Lunch—Students form groups of five; an odd student may join any group. Each group of five students sits in a circle, pretending to eat.
- Exercise—Students demonstrate their favorite exercise.
- Fire drill—Students line up in correct class order quietly. As an alternative, they can line up in alphabetical order by first or last name.
- Recreation—Students form groups of three and one student pretends to jump rope while two other students pretend to turn the rope.
- Rest—Students sit on the floor and check their pulses.

Variations

- Change some commands to include the use of gym scooters (one for each student). The following are some examples:

  - Train—Two or more students hold hands while moving on scooters.
  - Bus—Sitting on scooters, two or more students link up by holding the legs of the student directly behind them.
  - Car-Partner—One student lies on his belly on the scooter (car), while another, the driver, sits on another scooter and steers the car by grabbing the legs of his partner.

⑥ Truck—This variation uses three students in the same manner as the car, but two students steer one by each holding a leg.

⑥ Merry-go-round—Four or more students hold hands in a circle, and the scooters go around in imitation of a merry-go-round.

⑥ Travel—Students go anywhere on the island, but the scooter must not stop moving.

⑥ North City—Students go to a designated area on the north side of the play area.

⑥ South City—Students go to a designated area on the south side of the play area.

⑥ School—Students sit on scooters and line up in the center of the play area, facing forward, according to class lines or by alphabetical order of first or last name.

⑥ Doctor—Each student finds a partner, and they take turns checking each other's pulse using the radial artery (on the wrist, under the thumb).

⑥ Follow the Leader—Each student finds a partner, and they take turns following each other.

⑥ Snake—Students lie down on their bellies on scooters. One or two students hold the ankles of the student in front. The front student gives the back student or students a ride by pushing only with the arms.

⑥ Jog—Students turn over scooters, leave them on the floor, and jog throughout the island without touching any scooters.

⑥ Ball—Students get a ball and play scooter catch with one or two other students.

⑥ Tag—Students find a partner and play tag. When tagged, a student spins around in a circle three times and then goes after the partner.

⑥ Top—Students spin around on their scooters as if they were tops.

⑥ Partner swing—Students find a partner and perform an elbow swing.

⑥ Partner spin—Students hold both hands of a partner and spin around.

⑥ High five—Students give as many high fives as they can while moving around.

⑥ This game, with or without scooters, may be played for points. Score one point each time a student carries out a successful command. Take away one point for bumping into another student or going into the water (outside of the perimeter line in the gymnasium). The students count their own points.

Fitness Run
Ages 8 and up

Here is a game, based on the game Rainbow Run, that requires small groups to work really well together, incorporates all aspects of physical fitness, and integrates the curriculum.

Topics

- Aerobic endurance
- Muscular strength and endurance
- Flexibility
- Locomotor skills
- Mathematical computation and solving equations

Objectives

- Psychomotor—Perform various exercises using correct form.
- Cognitive—Solve simple equations or math examples; understand which exercises affect which parts of the body.
- Affective—Enjoy activities that promote fitness; work cooperatively with small groups to achieve success.

Equipment

- Several traffic cones
- Index cards to place under each cone
- 1 hula hoop or playground ball for each group

Safety

- Watch for other moving groups.
- Move carefully so that all members of your group will be able to easily stay together.

Game

1. Prior to the start of class, randomly place the traffic cones throughout the play area.
2. Place one index card with a fitness problem under each traffic cone. Here's an example: Push-ups: Solve for x: $x + 5 = 10$. Can you do x amount of push-ups? For younger students, substitute addition or subtraction examples.
3. A different fitness problem goes under each cone.

4. If there are seven cones with seven problems, the class divides into seven groups. If there are six cones, the class divides into six groups, and so forth.

5. Keep a master list in a definite order, such as an index card listing the following exercises in order (from the top to the bottom of the card), with the answer to the fitness problem beside each: Push-ups 5, Sit-ups 10, Jumping jacks 15, Crunches 14, and so forth.

6. Give each group a different exercise to find. Each member of the group must hold on to the hoop or put one hand on the ball. The group finds the stated exercise, solves the problem, does the exact number of repetitions, and reports to you, the teacher. The group stays attached at all times except when they are performing the exercises. When performing the exercises, the group should move away from the cone and find some empty space in order not to give away what is under each cone and to make room for other groups. They must not remove the index cards from underneath the cones.

7. When each group reports its last exercise total, give the group the name of the next exercise on the list, cycling back to the top of the list when a group gets to the end. If they just did sit-ups, they look next for jumping jacks; if they did jumping jacks, they look for crunches, and so forth.

8. Students try to complete all the exercises with the correct number of repetitions. If a group reports an incorrect amount, ask them to go back and redo the problem. If the answer is incorrect a second time, tell them the correct answer.

   ◎ Competitive—The first group to complete the entire course is the winner. Alternatively, this group may go back and start from the beginning to see how far it can get while the other groups finish. If time permits, rearrange the exercises and start again.

   ◎ Cooperative—The class tries to beat its best time.

Variations

◎ Vary the kinds of exercises.

◎ Vary the kinds of problems.

◎ Place more traffic cones than problems. Some cones will have nothing under them.

◎ For stretches, instead of repetitions, ask the students to do a given number of stretches.

◎ Use equipment to move with. For example, everyone dribbles a basketball.

Follow the Leader

Ages 4 to 7   **Ages 8 and up**

locomotor skills only   **equipment used**

Follow the Leader may be an old game, but this version allows for multiple leaders and constant movement. Tell the students they are going to play a new version of Follow the Leader. Young children love this game.

Topics

- ⚅ Aerobic endurance
- ⚅ Locomotor skills
- ⚅ Manipulative skills
- ⚅ Leadership and followership skills
- ⚅ Cooperation
- ⚅ Safety awareness

Objectives

- ⚅ Psychomotor—Move safely while performing locomotor skills in various directions, levels, and pathways.
- ⚅ Cognitive—Understand the approximate speed at which to move in order to maintain aerobic fitness.
- ⚅ Affective—Appreciate the cooperative nature of working with a partner; appreciate individual differences in ability.

Equipment

None, or 1 piece of equipment for each student

Safety

⚠ Move with control and look in the direction you are going.

Game

1. Divide the class into pairs or groups of three or four students.
2. In each pair or group, one student is the leader and the other student or students are the followers.
3. Students spread out in scatter formation.

4. The leader in each group begins to move throughout the play area using any designated locomotor movement except running (this would be a good time for the class to discuss why running is anaerobic and why it is not as safe as other locomotor skills). The leaders may change movement, direction, or level at any time.

5. The followers try to follow behind the leaders and imitate what they are doing.

6. After about a minute, give a predetermined signal to change leaders.

7. The second person in the pair or in line becomes the new leader, and the leader moves to the back.

Variations

◎ Students use a piece of equipment (ball, hoop, or rope).

◎ The students link a part of their bodies to each other.

◎ Any member of the group may request that the leader slow down the pace.

◎ For ages 8 and up, each group or pair may choreograph a sequence of skills, levels, and directions.

Gym Scooter Derby
Ages 4 and up

A great deal can be done with gym scooters. Here is a cluster of short games that are sure to keep the children moving and excited.

Topics

◎ Aerobic endurance

◎ Muscular strength and endurance

◎ Cooperation

◎ Safety awareness

Objectives

◎ Psychomotor—Demonstrate proficiency in manipulating a gym scooter in at least three ways.

◎ Cognitive—Recall movement patterns while manipulating a gym scooter; understand the game's fitness benefits.

◎ Affective—Enjoy scooter movement and obey safety rules.

Equipment

1 gym scooter for each student

Safety

- ⊚ Review rules for gym scooters.
- ⊚ Move with control.
- ⊚ Avoid collisions.

Game

1. Students spread out in scatter formation.
2. Ask a series of movement questions such as: "Can you sit, lie on your belly or chest, or kneel on one or both knees? From these body positions, can you move forward, backward, or sideways? Can you move slowly or at a medium speed? Can you make circles or other patterns on the floor?"

Variations

- ⊚ Follow the Leader—One partner follows another, then they switch leaders; at a given signal, everyone finds a new partner; everyone does what the leader is doing; or everyone silently chooses one or two students to follow without telling anyone whom they are following (when one person changes, it causes a whole chain reaction).

- ⊚ Statues—Say, "When the music stops or the whistle blows, how quickly can you make your scooter stop and freeze as if you were a statue?" Statues can freeze in various ways: happy, angry, sad, funny, tall, small, wide, thin, and so forth. They can also combine categories and freeze in more than one way (e.g., a small, happy statue).

- ⊚ Scooter Tag—The It or Its lie down on the scooter. Everyone else sits. The Its try to tag the sitting students lightly on the back. When tagged, a student either becomes another It (progressive tag), or gets off the scooter, turns it upside down, and remains still until someone who has not been tagged rides over and turns the scooter right-side up (infinity tag).

- ⊚ Clean Up the Gym—This is a good game for putting the scooters away at the end of the period. Hold a long, soft stick or tube and walk quickly. When you touch a student with the tube, that student must stand and carry the scooter to the designated cleanup area. The students try to get away from you.

- ⊚ Road and Track—Place traffic cones around the gymnasium to represent a track. The students all drive their scooters in the same direction around the track. If students have partners, one can be the pusher or driver. Vary the way the students ride on the scooters. When you call out to reverse, they must go the other way.

⑥ Vehicles—Students make groups according to the following commands: Cars—groups of two, Trucks—groups of three, Buses—groups of four, Trains—groups of five or six. The students move around attached to each other.

Keep-Away Scooter Ball
Ages 8 and up

Children love to play Keep-Away. This version uses gym scooters for muscular strength and endurance.

Topics

⑥ Muscular strength and endurance

⑥ Manipulative skills

Objectives

⑥ Psychomotor—Manipulate several kinds of balls while riding on a scooter.

⑥ Cognitive—Understand the application of force necessary to control the ball while riding on a gym scooter; understand the fitness aspect of the game.

⑥ Affective—Appreciate individual differences in ability.

Equipment

⑥ Various kinds of balls

⑥ 1 scooter for each student

Safety

⑥ Review gym scooter rules.

⑥ Remind the students to always look in the direction they are going.

Game

1. Students spread out in scatter formation.

2. Each student receives one scooter.

3. Choose about one-fourth of the class to put the balls away into a bag. These students lie down on their scooters.

4. The rest of the students sit on their scooters.

5. Distribute various kinds of balls to the students who are sitting on the scooters.

6. On the go signal, the students who are trying to put the balls away attempt to tag any student with a ball. If tagged while in possession of a ball, a student must hand it to the tagger, who takes the ball, scoots to a bag, and puts it away.

7. Students sitting on a scooter may pass the balls to each other or just roll them away. Any student, including a tagger, may pick up a loose ball.

8. Note that as more balls are put away, passing increases.

9. Time the event. When all the balls are put away, announce the time and choose new students to put the balls away.

10. Physical contact is prohibited except for tagging.

Variations

◎ Use only one type of ball.

◎ Use soccer balls. The students sitting on scooters may use only their feet to keep the balls away from the taggers. Upon capturing a loose ball, taggers may stand with their scooters and walk to the bag.

◎ Use beach balls. The students sitting on scooters may strike the ball only with their hands to keep the ball away from the taggers. The taggers may stand with their scooters and walk to the bag.

◎ Progressive—Choose only one or two taggers. When a student is tagged and loses her ball, she becomes a tagger. Play until one or two balls are left. The last student (or two) with a ball becomes the new tagger (or taggers) in the next round.

Movement Partners
Ages 5 and up

Young children really enjoy this game. The children are encouraged to work with many classmates while practicing their movement skills. Always encourage the children to work with everyone. Because of the short amount of time spent with each partner, children do not feel trapped working with someone whom they might find difficult.

Topics

◎ Aerobic endurance

◎ Locomotor skills

◎ Cooperation

Objectives

- Psychomotor—Demonstrate several locomotor skills; quickly find a partner or small group.
- Cognitive—Identify locomotor skills; identify changes in the body during physical activity.
- Affective—Cooperate with a partner or group; enjoy participating in a variety of movement activities.

Equipment

None, or a variety of equipment such as balls or beanbags

Safety

- Move with control.
- Watch where your group is going.

Game

1. Students spread out in scatter formation.
2. Ask the students to move throughout the play area in a variety of ways: "Can you skip around the gymnasium and, when I say, 'Partner,' can you join hands with one other person and continue skipping?" If handholding presents a problem, each student may have a small piece of rope to hold.
3. Each new question requires a new partner or small group.
4. Use any kind of signal for the students to find a new partner. Vary the locomotor skills and the number of partners. Encourage the students to find a partner or group close by (one way to encourage quick partners is to change questions quickly so that students who do not find a partner miss the chance to link up).

Variations

- The students find a partner who meets a specific requirement: "Find a partner who is wearing the same color of socks as you."
- After finding a partner, students perform other activities with that partner. For example, one partner forms a bridge and the other partner goes under the bridge. Or if students are using equipment, one partner gets a ball and the partners play catch with the ball.
- Both partners perform the same activity, such as lying facedown next to each other and taking turns rolling over each other.

◎ Partners use equipment and play Follow the Leader, Partner Tag, or Invent a Routine, or they just move with their partner.

◎ Here are some suggested questions:

◎ Can you find a partner near your height?

◎ Can you find a partner who is wearing a color of sneakers (or any other piece of clothing) similar to yours?

◎ Can you choose a partner by walking and placing your hands lightly on another person's shoulders? Continue walking. Can you link up with two other people to form a group of four?

◎ Can you tag someone lightly? Can you and your partner tag another pair lightly?

No-Relay Relay
Ages 5 and up

Relay races tend to focus on the product (winning) and not the process (learning new skills, practicing learned skills, or fitness). They are also difficult to organize and hard to judge. No-Relay Relay addresses these problems and turns the old relay race into a fun, educational, and fitness-oriented game.

Topics

◎ Aerobic endurance

◎ Muscular strength and endurance

◎ Locomotor skills

◎ Manipulative skills

◎ Cooperation

Objectives

◎ Psychomotor—Be able to demonstrate several kinds of movement forms; manipulate equipment while moving.

◎ Cognitive—Identify and understand the game's fitness focus; understand force as it applies to moving an object accurately.

◎ Affective—Appreciate individual differences in ability; cooperate with small teams to achieve success.

Equipment

None, or many kinds

Safety

⚠ ⦿ Move with control.

⦿ When throwing an object, aim carefully.

Game

1. The class divides into small teams of three to five students.
2. The teams line up behind a designated starting line.
3. One traffic cone or marker for each team is placed at the other end of the play area.
4. On the go signal, the first player from each team uses a designated loco-motor skill to go around the marker and back. The team counts one point every time a member completes one turn.
5. Students play for a designated amount of time.
6. They then play again. Each team tries to beat its previous score.

Variations

⦿ Vary the locomotor skills.

⦿ Play any known relay race in this manner.

⦿ Place a ball on top of the traffic cone. One person places the ball on the traffic cone; the next person takes it off.

⦿ Place one tennis can or bowling pin on a poly spot at one end of the play area. Give a beanbag to the first team member in line. He slides the beanbag at the target can or pin. If he knocks it down, the team gets two points; he then runs and sets up the target again and hands the beanbag to the next person. If he does not knock down the target he tags the next person in line, who runs to where the beanbag stopped and slides it from that point. Play continues until a player knocks down the target. Then the team counts one point and that player resets the target, runs back, and hands the beanbag to the next person on line.

⦿ Place a hoop at one end of the play area and proceed as in the previous variation, except that students try to toss a beanbag into the hoop. Remember that in both games no player may ever move with the beanbag in hand until after the objective is reached. At that point the player retrieves the beanbag and runs it back to the next person. Do not allow the students to throw the beanbag back to the next person in line unless you specifically tell them they can.

⦿ Instead of running the beanbag back, students slide or toss it back and then run back to the line.

- Place one poly spot for each team at the far end of the play area. Begin with one member from each team standing on this spot. One foot must always be on the poly spot.
    - Give one type of tossing, striking, or throwing implement to the first person in each line.
    - On the go signal, this person tries to toss, throw, or strike the implement toward the team member on the poly spot. The intent is for the person on the poly spot to catch the implement.
    - Play continues as in the previous variations until the person on the spot catches the implement. At that point, the person who last threw the implement changes places with the poly spot person. The person who caught the implement runs it back to the next person in line and then moves to the end of the line.
    - Teams count one point for each catch.
    - Designate whether the implement must be caught on the fly or on a certain number of bounces.
- Competitive—Keep track of which team scored the most points.
- Cooperative—Each team tries to beat its best score.
- Cooperative—Total all scores and see whether the entire class can beat its best score.
- After each round, one member of each team rotates to a new team.

Now
Ages 8 and up

Here is another version of the game Collection (see page 28). The game Now is a more individual game but is also very aerobic. It also gives the students a lot of practice with eye–hand coordination.

Topics

- Aerobic endurance
- Locomotor skills
- Manipulative skills
- Cooperation
- Safety awareness

Objectives

- Psychomotor—Demonstrate the ability to manipulate a tennis or soft-type ball while performing various locomotor skills.

⊚ Cognitive—Formulate strategies for moving quickly and safely.

⊚ Affective—Appreciate individual differences in ability; cooperate to move safely and to achieve success as a group.

Equipment

1 tennis or soft-type ball for each student

Safety

⊚ Move with control.

⊚ Watch for collisions with other students.

Game

1. Each student receives one ball.

2. Students spread out in scatter formation.

3. The students demonstrate various locomotor skills while manipulating the balls in various ways according to your prompts: "Can you skip throughout the play area while tossing and catching your ball?" "Can you jog throughout the play area while bouncing and catching your ball?"

4. Explain that tossing and catching a piece of equipment while moving requires extra safety precautions.

5. When you say, "Now!" the students roll the ball away. Or, in the case of a soft-type ball, they may toss it up and away and pick up someone else's ball. As soon as students pick up a ball, they immediately begin tossing and catching again.

Variations

⊚ When tossing and catching a ball, the students count one point for each successful catch. This variation encourages students to pick up a new ball quickly and see how high a score they can get in 2 to 3 minutes. Then they play again and try to beat their previous individual scores.

⊚ Each student has a partner or is in a small group of three or four. On your signal, the partners attempt to play catch with each other.

⊚ When students are using partners, you occasionally give a different signal to find new partners.

⊚ Students use a different kind of ball and practice a different skill. For example, students dribble a soccer ball with the feet. At the signal, the students push the soccer ball away and trap a different ball. They immediately begin to dribble the new ball.

⊚ Cooperative—Time the students to see how long it takes before everyone is working with a new ball; ask the students to try to beat that time in the next round.

Partner Scooters
Ages 8 and up

Scooters are wonderful for building muscular strength and endurance. It is always a good idea to change partners a few times during the lesson.

Topics

- Aerobic endurance
- Muscular strength and endurance
- Manipulative skills
- Cooperation

Objectives

- Psychomotor—Demonstrate several ways to manipulate a gym scooter and demonstrate manipulative skills using at least three kinds of balls.
- Cognitive—Understand the fitness aspects of the game.
- Affective—Appreciate individual differences in ability.

Equipment

- 1 gym scooter for each student
- Several kinds of balls

Safety

- Review the rules for gym scooters.
- Remind students to look for the empty spaces, especially when racing.

Game

1. Each student receives one gym scooter.
2. Students choose a partner according to skill level, one they think is fairly equal in athletic ability. If one student is left over, that student chooses any pair and forms a group of three. You may also choose the partners for the students.
3. Students play several partner games.
   - The students choose a way to ride the scooters and race each other. If one student wins three races in a row, that student finds a new partner.
   - Each pair of students chooses a ball. They attempt to work the ball from one side of the gymnasium to the other by passing it. They may

either sit or lie on the scooter. The person with the ball cannot move and must stop until he throws it to his partner.

⑥ Set two goals on either end of the gymnasium. Place various kinds of balls at one end of the gymnasium in a container. Place an empty container on the other end. The students try to move all the balls from one container to the other and may work either individually or in pairs. They may sit or lie on the scooters. The person with the ball cannot move and must throw back and forth with her partner or, if playing individually, with anyone without a ball. Time the event, and students see whether they can beat their best time. They may try various methods of accomplishing this task. Then you may pick one and ask all the students to use the same method.

⑥ The game can proceed as previously described, but with some students acting as disrupters. The disrupters lie on their scooters and attempt to tag any student with a ball. If tagged while in possession of a ball, a student must replace the ball in the original basket or, as a variation, hand the ball to the disrupter, who then takes it back to the original basket. In this variation, the disrupters sit on their scooters. As another variation the disrupters, sitting on their scooters, can place the balls in their own containers. These containers may be placed at the two sides of the gymnasium along the centerline.

Return the Fitness Favor
Ages 8 and up

If someone does you a favor, you usually try to return it. In this game the children try to help each other by knocking down something someone else owns. When your object is knocked down, you get to do some exercise. This game requires a lot of strategy. Let students figure out their own strategies.

Topics

⑥ Aerobic endurance

⑥ Muscular strength and endurance

⑥ Manipulative skills

⑥ Cooperation

⑥ Strategy

Objectives

⑥ Psychomotor—Slide beanbags accurately, toss or throw balls accurately, and perform simple exercises with correct form.

◎ Cognitive—Understand correct form of exercises; understand how each exercise benefits a fitness category; understand the game's strategy.

◎ Affective—Play the game honestly.

Equipment

◎ 1 covered tennis ball can with 1, 2, 3, or no balls inside; 1 bowling pin (with at least four colors of pins available); or 1 small traffic cone (with at least four colors available) per student

◎ 1 or 2 beanbags per student

◎ Some fleece or other soft-type balls

◎ 5 or 6 jump ropes

Safety

◎ Aim low and at the targets when throwing a ball.

◎ Make sure the beanbag slides on the ground and does not fly up in the air.

Game

1. Explain to the students that the object of the game is to return a fitness favor to anyone who helps them become fit. Or they may help anyone else become fit.

2. Each student receives one of the following: a covered tennis can with one, two, three, or no balls inside; one bowling pin (various colors available); or one small plastic traffic cone (various colors available).

3. Each student also receives one or two beanbags.

4. Students spread out in scatter formation. The corners of the play area are left empty; they will be used for exercises.

5. The students set up their cones, pins, or cans in their own personal space. The traffic cones should be set upside down.

6. After the game begins, toss some balls out into general space.

7. The object of the game is for students to slide the beanbags or throw the balls so that they knock down someone else's cone, pin, or can and help them become fit. They may not knock down a pin or traffic cone of the same color as theirs or a can with the same amount of tennis balls in it as theirs.

8. If a student's object is knocked down, she leaves it down, goes to a corner of the play area, and performs a fitness activity. One corner may be for curl-ups, one corner for push-ups, one corner for ski jumps, and one corner for jumping ropes.

9. After performing a set number of repetitions (set the number for each exercise depending on the age and ability of the class), the student either returns to her object, resets it, and begins play or moves to a new location in the play area and resets the object. She may want to return the favor to the person who knocked down her object.

10. Every time students' objects are knocked down, they go to a different corner. After four times, they may choose any corner.

11. A student may only protect his object with his feet; he must be standing up. If he knocks down his object himself, he must perform an exercise. If someone with the same color of pin or cone knocks down his object, that player should tell him to set it back up.

12. Students may stay near their object or venture away. However, if they move away from their object, they must constantly check back to see whether it is still standing. Most students try to stay near their object, sliding the beanbags and throwing the balls from that spot. They generally move only slightly away to try to get a new piece of equipment. Remind them that the strategy is up to them.

Variations

◎ Vary the exercise stations or the number of repetitions.

◎ Allow the students to choose their own individual number of repetitions of an exercise. This would be a good time to explain the FITT principle, particularly intensity (the more repetitions, the more intensity).

◎ Vary the equipment used to knock down the objects.

◎ Have a couple of special pieces of equipment such as beach balls. If a student's object is knocked down by one of these special pieces of equipment, that student must go to two different corners before returning to the game.

Scrabble Fitness
Ages 7 and up*

*(ages 5 and 6 to find letters or numbers
and place them in numerical or alphabetical order)*

Scrabble is a nice, quiet word game. But this game demands that the students move; it requires quickness, agility, and stamina. Students need reading, spelling, and even math skills to play the game well.

Topics

- Aerobic endurance
- Cooperation
- Teamwork
- Reading, spelling, and math skills

Objectives

- Psychomotor—Show agility, speed, and endurance.
- Cognitive—Understand the best way to start, stop, bend, and reach; understand the game's fitness benefits; form words using letters.
- Affective—Appreciate individual differences in ability; cooperate to keep the game moving and safe.

Equipment

- 75 or more index cards, cardboard squares, or tennis balls with individual letters written on each
- A hoop for each team

Safety

Remind the students to avoid collisions in the center circle area.

Game

1. Scatter the index cards facedown in the center circle of the play area. If the area has no lines, create a circle with poly spots.
2. Divide the class into teams of three. If there are extra students, one or two teams can have four.
3. Each team receives one hoop.
4. The teams place the hoops around the center circle, 15 to 20 feet (4.5 to 6 meters) away from the middle.
5. The teams establish an order of running and stand in that order next to their hoop.
6. On the go signal, the first person from each team runs to the center circle, picks one card without looking at the letter, runs back, and places the card faceup in the hoop. As soon as the card is placed in the hoop, the next runner goes.
7. The game continues until there are no more cards in the center circle.
8. The teams get 2 to 3 minutes to form as many words as they can. The words may or may not be connected to each other as in Scrabble.
9. Students may form words by using the letters both up and down, as in Scrabble.
10. The team with the most words is the winner of that round.

⚡Variations

- ⑥ Place point values on letters, as in Scrabble. Add up the points.
- ⑥ Give more points for longer words, such as one point for each letter used in a word. Therefore, a five-letter word gets five points.
  - ⑥ Cooperative—Total all the class points. Play again and see whether the class can score more points in the next round.
- ⑥ Scatter tennis balls or cardboard squares with letters written on them all over the play area. All players may move at the same time. Each player can pick up only one letter at a time. A player must place that ball or cardboard square inside her team's hoop before searching for a new letter. When all the balls or cards are in the hoops, players have 2 to 3 minutes to form as many words as possible. Play competitively, team versus team, or play cooperatively and total all scores. Repeat the round.
- ⑥ Instead of letters, place facts or statements on the cards. Spread the cards out facedown throughout the play area. Each team is given a list of facts or statements to find. Players find all their designated facts or statements. If a player turns over a card that the team does not need, the player leaves it facedown, does one jumping jack, and returns to tag the next team member.
- ⑥ Distribute paragraphs with missing words to each team. Players find the missing words, which are placed facedown throughout the play area.
- ⑥ For ages 5 and 6, place index cards or use tennis balls with letters or numbers written on them. The game is played with everyone moving at once, but students may pick up only one ball or card at a time. After all the balls or cards are taken, the teams place them in numerical or alphabetical order. They can also place them in reverse order. Additionally, they may take two balls or cards with numbers on them, add them, and see whether they have another ball or card that matches their answer. They can make simple three- or four-letter words out of the lettered balls or cards.

Spaghetti, Spaghetti, Meatball Parachute

Ages 4 and up

Imagine Duck Duck Goose as a fitness game. This version gives the arms and shoulders a great workout.

⚡Topics

- ⑥ Muscular strength and endurance
- ⑥ Locomotor skills
- ⑥ Cooperation

Objectives

- ◎ Psychomotor—Cooperatively shake a parachute at various speeds.
- ◎ Cognitive—Understand the fitness benefits of the game; understand how to communicate as a group.
- ◎ Affective—Work cooperatively to keep the game moving.

Equipment

1 parachute

Safety

Remind students that tags are light touches, never pushes.

Game

1. The students find a place around the outside of the parachute.
2. They practice shaking the parachute, making both soft waves and vigorous waves. Ask which way requires more work.
3. Choose one student to be It. He walks around the outside of the parachute and taps each student on the shoulder while saying, "Spaghetti." The students are making soft gentle waves. When It says, "Meatball," the tapped student (the meatball) lets go of the parachute and gives chase around the outside. Meanwhile, the rest of the students shake the parachute vigorously, making fast waves.
4. While the chute is shaking vigorously, the meatball continues the chase until she catches It or until the group decides to make gentle waves.
5. When the waves turn gentle, if It has not been caught, he tries to get into the meatball's vacated spot before being tagged.
6. If the meatball catches It, she has the option of becoming the new It or returning to her spot.
7. The game continues with the new It walking around the parachute.

Variations

- ◎ Vary the locomotor skills.
- ◎ The students holding the parachute may drop one hand from the parachute and, using a chosen locomotor skill, move in unison in the opposite direction to the two runners.
- ◎ If the students lift the parachute to make a mushroom, the It may go under the parachute and out the other side. The chaser must stay on the outside.

- If the students pull back on the chute, making it stop, the It may reverse directions.
- Choose one person to be the leader. That person will control what the chute is doing. Change leaders often. Don't use this option unless the students are having a lot of difficulty communicating. One of the main objectives of this game is teaching communication skills.
- Use two parachutes. Play two simultaneous games. When an It is caught, he moves to the other parachute.

Trick or Treat
Ages 7 and up

This game was created for Halloween, but use it any time of the year by simply changing the name. The game uses gym scooters and involves some manipulative skills as well as teamwork.

Topics

- Aerobic endurance
- Muscular strength and endurance
- Manipulative skills
- Teamwork
- Cooperation

Objectives

- Psychomotor—Be able to show two ways to ride a gym scooter; change direction and speed on a scooter; slide a beanbag accurately.
- Cognitive—Understand the game's strategy; understand the fitness aspects of the game.
- Affective—Play fairly and honestly.

Equipment

- Approximately 1 gym scooter for every two students
- 10 to 20 beanbags
- 50 to 75 tennis balls
- 1 hoop or container for every two students
- 3 or 4 hoops to hold the rest of the tennis balls
- Traffic cones or poly spots for line markers

Safety

⚠ ◎ Review safety rules for gym scooters.

◎ Remind the students that when they walk with a gym scooter, they should tuck it under their arms and move slowly so as not to bump into riders.

Game

1. Tell the students they are going trick-or-treating. The tennis balls are the treats. They have to cross a dark, scary field and get past monsters to get to the treats.

2. Place tennis balls in three or four hoops, which are spread out on one end of the play area.

3. The students each have a partner and share one scooter, on the opposite end of the play area from where the tennis balls are located.

4. Three monsters (students on scooters) are in the half of the play area closest to the tennis balls. However, designate a safety area near the tennis balls with a taped line, traffic cones, or poly spots. The monsters may not go into the safety area or cross the centerline. They may, however, cross the centerline to retrieve beanbags; they may not slide the beanbags until they return to the monster area.

5. Spread out the beanbags on the monster side of the play area.

6. The monsters lie on their bellies on the scooters. The children sit on their scooters. On the go signal, one of the two partners attempts to cross into the monster area, get past the monsters, pick up one treat (tennis ball) and get back to his partner. If successful, he places the tennis ball in a hoop or container and gives the scooter to his partner.

7. The monsters attempt to pick up a beanbag and slide it at the wheels or at the student's feet. A beanbag that goes under the wheels is considered a hit, whether or not it comes out the other side. If the wheels or feet are hit, the student stands and carries the scooter back to her partner. The monster must verbally inform if a hit is made; sometimes children don't realize that a beanbag touched or went under their scooter. Now it's the partner's turn to go. If a player is carrying a tennis ball when hit, she drops the ball on the floor. It may be picked up by anyone at a later time.

8. Once the children leave the monster side of the play area, they are safe.

9. Play for about 5 minutes, replace the tennis balls in their original hoops, and pick new monsters.

Variations

◎ Instead of having partners, everyone receives a scooter and a container or hoop to hold the treats. If hit or tagged, they must return to their container and begin again.

- Competitive—The pair or individual who collected the most treats (tennis balls) is the winner.
- Cooperative—Count the total number of tennis balls collected. Try to beat this score in the next round.
- Instead of sliding beanbags, the monsters tag the children.

Wheelbarrow Challenge
Ages 8 and up

Remember how partners got into a wheelbarrow position? The game was usually played as wheelbarrow races. Here are variations that give the arms and shoulders a great workout.

Topics

- Muscular strength and endurance
- Locomotor skills
- Cooperation

Objectives

- Psychomotor—Be able to maintain a wheelbarrow position for a minimum of 1 minute while performing various tasks.
- Cognitive—Understand how to work with a partner to maintain balance; judge the size and strength of others.
- Affective—Work cooperatively with partners to perform tasks successfully.

Equipment

None, or beanbags, hoops, or other small equipment

Safety

- Avoid collisions.
- Take a brief rest if very tired.
- Practice the wheelbarrow position until all the children feel comfortable with it. If one child is not strong enough to support his partner, switch partners.

Game

1. Ask the students to find a partner who is approximately equal in size and strength. A student without a partner becomes a judge for one round and then rotates with another student.

2. See whether the students can maintain the wheelbarrow position. One student assumes a push-up position; the other student lifts the partner's legs by grasping the ankles and moves between the feet, thus forming a human wheelbarrow.

3. Have the students practice moving throughout the play area. Make sure each student has a turn at the two positions.

4. Play any of the following variations. Allow students to rest, if necessary, during any of these games.

Variations

- ⊚ Hockey—Each twosome receives a beanbag. As the students move around, they try to slide the beanbag under the body of another wheelbarrow and out the other side. Alternatively, they can try to face another twosome and slide the beanbag between the two arms of the other team. Either way, they must retrieve their beanbag before they continue the game. The students may switch positions at any time. Score one point for each success.

- ⊚ Cooperative Musical Hoops—Hoops, one for each twosome, are scattered around the play area. When the music is playing, the students move around in wheelbarrow fashion. When the music stops, each wheelbarrow must get a body part into a hoop. After each stoppage of music, decrease the number of hoops by one.

- ⊚ Transport—The students start at one end of the play area or at a designated starting line. Place small equipment like beanbags or hoops on the other end. The students must transport the objects from one end to the other. They may take only one object at a time. They carry the object any way they wish. Alternatively, designate a body part with which to carry the object.

  - ⊚ Cooperative—Time the students. After they've rested a short time, ask them to try to beat the last recorded time.

  - ⊚ Competitive—See which pair transports the most objects.

- ⊚ Tag—Any student in the push-up position can tag any other student. If tagged, the student in the push-up position changes places with her partner.

- ⊚ Change Partners—Play some music. When the music stops, everyone must find a new partner.

- ⊚ Wheelbarrow Dance—Students work in groups of two wheelbarrows (four students). Each group choreographs a short wheelbarrow dance to music.

Zombie Ball
Ages 8 and up

This game was created for Halloween, but use it at any other time of the year by simply changing the name or the locomotor skills. Zombie Ball is the kind of game that lends itself to some students not playing fairly. In this game, you may find that some students try to get touched by the ball in order to become a zombie. If this should happen, discuss the idea that trying to be tagged or touched on purpose is a form of cheating, because that is not the intention of the game. Explain how this behavior nullifies the game if people act in this manner.

Topics

- Aerobic endurance
- Locomotor skills
- Manipulative skills
- Cooperation
- Teamwork

Objectives

- Psychomotor—Be able to roll a ball with control and accuracy; dodge a rolling ball.
- Cognitive—Understand the application of force when rolling a ball for accuracy; understand the strategy of a group game situation.
- Affective—Cooperate to keep the game moving and safe; play fairly and honestly.

Equipment

1 playground or foam-type ball for every two or three students.

Safety

- Avoid collisions.
- Look in the direction you are going.
- Move with control.
- Keep the ball on the ground.

Game

1. Tell the students that they are all trapped in a haunted house, and there is no escape. There is also one zombie in the house. The area of the haunted house should be about the size of a basketball court. Use the lines in the gymnasium or place traffic cones around the perimeter of the play area.

2. The humans may not leave the haunted house (go outside the lines or cones). A zombie may leave the house to retrieve a ball.

3. The zombie begins the game with a ball. The zombie moves with arms out, taking large walking steps and holding the ball in one or both hands. The humans may choose any locomotor skill.

4. The humans must try their best to remain humans for as long as possible.

5. The zombie attempts to roll the ball at the feet of the humans. If a human is hit on the foot or feet (must be below the knee), the human becomes a zombie. The zombie may retrieve the ball he just rolled or go to the zombie ball area (a place just outside the haunted house) and get another ball. The new zombie goes to the zombie ball area and picks up a zombie ball. If there are no more balls, the zombies may pick up any loose ball. The humans may never touch a zombie ball.

6. Play continues until all humans are turned into zombies, or for about 4 to 5 minutes. The last human left is declared the winner. If timing the game, after 5 minutes, any humans still left may be declared the winners.

7. Start a new round of Zombie Ball. The winner may become, or choose, the next zombie.

Variations

◉ Allow only one kind of locomotor skill for the humans.

◉ A zombie can be turned human again if hit by another zombie. Only the original zombie may never become human.

◉ Start the game with one-third of the class as zombies. Place two or three balls that are different from the zombie balls in the haunted house. In this version, when a human is hit, she freezes. She may be unfrozen by another human who picks up a human ball and rolls the ball so that it touches the frozen human's feet. Play for 3 to 4 minutes. If there are any humans left, the humans are the winners. Choose new zombies.

◉ Change the name of the game. For example, in Turkey Trot, the turkeys trot and gobble. They try to turn the humans into turkeys so that they will not be eaten on Thanksgiving.

◉ Cooperative—Time the event or play 3-minute rounds. See how long it takes all the humans to become zombies, or see how many humans are left after 3 minutes. See whether the humans can do better next time.

Tag Games

Tag games are great exercise motivators. They are generally extremely active and therefore very useful for aerobic fitness. When you add equipment, the students also receive greatly needed fundamental skill practice. Tag games that encourage children to move freely in space provide the additional benefit of teaching spatial awareness. These games also make good warm-up activities, particularly if the tag game relates to the lesson to follow.

Numerous variations of tag exist. Below are six categories. Equipment is optional; however, it is a good idea to give the taggers a tagging implement. For example, tagging with a soft foam ball or a soft foam Frisbee helps easily identify the taggers and encourages them to make a soft and safe tag.

Here are the six categories of tag:

1. Remedy tag (often called freeze or infinity tag)—This type of tag game allows the tagged student to reenter the game. Choose about 10 percent of the students to be Its. Give the Its a tagging tool or let them wear something identifiable such as pinnies. When tagged, the students freeze. Other students may unfreeze them in various ways. Some examples are giving a high five, crawling between the legs of the frozen student (ages 5 to 7 love this variation), shaking hands, performing an elbow swing, and so on. Play for 1 to 3 minutes and then switch Its. In most cases, allow immunity for the students who are freeing frozen students. Say the following: "When you are helping another child, you cannot be tagged." Review the vocabulary *immunity* and *remedy*.

2. Progressive tag—One student begins as the It. To identify the It, this student moves in a different way from the rest of the students. For example, the It walks, whereas everyone else skips or gallops. Tagged students become Its. They change to the way the It moves. Play continues until all of the students become Its. The last student tagged becomes the first It in the next game. In any progressive tag game, the danger exists that students will try to be tagged on purpose because they want to become an It. Discuss with your students that trying to be tagged on purpose is a form of cheating, because this behavior does not conform to the spirit of the game. However, during the game, ignore the students who still try to get tagged and speak privately with them at a later time.

3. Safety tag—This form of tag allows students a way to be safe from being tagged. For example, they may be safe while kneeling or assuming the push-up position. They may be safe if they join hands with another student. They may be safe if they are performing jumping jacks. They may be safe if they are standing on something (line or poly spot) or in something (hoop). As in remedy tag, choose about 10 percent of the students to be It. Safety tag is generally a slower game, because many children will spend periods of time not moving. Discuss the aerobic consequences of remaining still. Although safety tag is less aerobic than some other games, it offers the children a chance to think strategically.

4. Cooperative tag—Students work together in various ways. For example, students form a group of four. Three of the students form a triangle and join hands. From outside of the triangle, the fourth student tries to tag a designated member of the triangle. The triangle moves to prevent the tag. After each tag, rotate positions.

   • Variation (blob tag)—Two students begin as Its. They join hands or link in some other way. When they tag another student, he joins on. After at least four players are linked, they may stay together or break into smaller groups.

   • Variation—Form lines of four to six. Each student holds the waist of the student in front. The first student in the line attempts to tag the last student in any other line. After each tag, the tagger rotates to the back of her line.

5. Quick tag—Divide the group into four or more teams. The teams stay within their own boundaries, which can be defined by gymnasium lines, traffic cones, or poly spots. One or two students from each team go into another team's territory so that each team has an equal amount of opponents. They become the Its. On the go signal, they try to tag everyone in this territory as quickly as possible. When tagged, students freeze. The first taggers to freeze all

opponents in one quadrant are the winners. Change Its and begin again.

- Variation—Time each round. See how long it takes the taggers to freeze all of the students. See which team of taggers uses the least amount of time. If using this variation, you can opt to play the game in one general space instead of using the four quadrants. As in the team version, use four or eight taggers.

6. Line tag—In these games, children must run from one line to another. The tagger or taggers are generally in the middle of the play area. In most games, the tagged player becomes a helper and tries to tag others. These games generally end when all or most of the players have been tagged. You can find many examples of this kind of tag game in other game books and on the Internet. I have purposely not placed any line tag games in this book because they do not teach spatial awareness, they are too teacher directed, they involve too much stop-and-go movement, and they are extremely dangerous (children tend to chase each other at full speed toward a line or wall).

You should discuss safety with students before playing each tag game. Instruct them to move with control. Most accidents occur because someone is moving too fast for the situation. Teach students to look in the direction they are going. Demonstrate that if they want to see who is behind them, they should stop and turn around instead of turning around while moving forward. Running may not be an option, depending on the skill level of the group. Have students use another locomotor skill. They can skip, walk, gallop, or slide. Teach students to tag gently and specify what body parts are eligible to be tagged.

Alien Remedy Tag
Ages 5 and up

Providing an atmosphere of fantasy enhances the enjoyment of this game. Define the words *alien* and *remedy*.

Topics

- Aerobic endurance
- Locomotor skills
- Manipulative skills
- Cooperation
- Safety awareness

Objectives

- ⊚ Psychomotor—Move safely while combining skipping, galloping, or walking with accurate throwing skills.
- ⊚ Cognitive—Understand and be able to explain the fitness benefits of the game.
- ⊚ Affective—Cooperate to achieve the common goal of playing honestly while keeping the game moving and safe.

Equipment

Foam balls, foam Frisbees, or other soft types of equipment

Safety

Remind the students to look in the direction they are going, move with control, and tag softly.

Game

1. Choose 10 to 20 percent of the students to be aliens from another planet or galaxy. The rest of the students are humans.
2. Each alien has a power freeze ray (a foam or sponge ball or any soft object).
3. Scatter one remedy pill for every two aliens (foam balls of a different color or size).
4. The humans are spread out throughout the play area (planet Earth). The aliens are behind a designated line, pretending to travel through space. Begin the game by announcing, "The aliens have landed and they're coming after you." The children generally start screaming as if they are scared. At this signal the aliens begin to skip, gallop, or walk after the humans. The humans skip, gallop, or walk away from the aliens.
5. The aliens freeze the humans by tagging them with their foam balls.
6. A frozen human may be unfrozen if another human picks up a remedy pill and throws the pill so that the frozen human can catch it. The human must keep both feet from moving while catching the remedy pill. If a human is tagged while holding the pill, he drops it and freezes.
7. Give the aliens 1 to 2 minutes to freeze all the humans.
8. The aliens may never touch the remedy pills, and the humans may never touch the power freeze balls.
9. At the conclusion of a round (1 to 2 minutes), the players walk around and deliver the remedy pills to you or another designated leader. Each alien chooses a new player to become an alien by handing the power freeze ray to that player. As soon as all the new aliens are aboard the space ship,

begin the next round. Make sure everyone who wants to be an alien has a chance to be one before anyone is chosen twice.

Variations

- ◎ Vary the locomotor skills.
- ◎ Instead of throwing the remedy pills, allow the students to give the pills to frozen students (especially for ages 5 to 7).
- ◎ Instead of using remedy pills, a human may free any frozen human by performing a designated task; for example, perform an elbow swing, shake hands, or join another human and place arms around the frozen human while chanting, "One, two, three, human free." Sometimes humans may be given a choice. For example, if a human is frozen and would like to be freed by only one human, she stands with legs wide so that the human may crawl through her legs (from the front only to prevent collisions). But if a human doesn't want anyone crawling through her legs, she stands with legs together so that two humans will free her by holding hands and chanting, "One, two, three, human free."

Basketball Dribble Tag
Ages 8 and up

Although dribble tag is not an original game, these variations will provide some exciting ways to practice dribbling while improving aerobic fitness.

Topics

- ◎ Aerobic endurance
- ◎ Locomotor skills
- ◎ Manipulative skills
- ◎ Cooperation

Objectives

- ◎ Psychomotor—Be able to dribble a basketball while changing speed and direction; use either hand to dribble a basketball.
- ◎ Cognitive—Understand the need to keep one's head up and switch hands, directions, and speed while dribbling a basketball; understand the game's aerobic fitness benefits.
- ◎ Affective—Appreciate the variations in ball-handling ability; cooperate by moving safely in general space.

Equipment

- 1 basketball for every 3 or 4 students or 1 basketball for each student (or playground balls as substitutes)
- 4 or 5 foam or fleece balls

Safety

- Remind the students that they may run only when in possession of a basketball.
- Because dribbling requires controlling the ball, they will not be able to move at full speed.
- Remind students to move with control.

Game

1. Distribute one basketball and one foam or fleece ball to every group of three or four students.
2. Students who are not in possession of a basketball may use any locomotor skill except running.
3. The student in each group with the basketball and a foam or fleece ball is It.
4. Students without a ball move away from the It.
5. On the go signal, the student with the basketball tries to tag the other two or three students in the group. When tagged, students freeze.
6. The student with the basketball dribbles at all times. Time each round for 2 to 3 minutes.

Variations

- Distribute two or three basketballs to each group. The student without the ball is It. The It may use any locomotor skill except running. When a tag is made, the tagged student becomes the new It and gives the basketball to the one who just tagged him. This variation is more aerobic, since everyone is in constant motion.
- Distribute basketballs to approximately one-third of the class. The students with the basketballs attempt to tag anyone without a ball. A tagged student freezes but may reenter the game if unfrozen by another student, who uses any acceptable method of unfreezing (such as giving the frozen student a high five or shaking hands with the frozen student). Play for 4 to 5 minutes and then choose a new third of the class to be the Its. To make the game more aerobic, instead of freezing, give the basketball to the tagged student, who becomes the new tagger. Play for 2 to 3 minutes and then start a new round, with different children beginning the game as Its.

⦾ Distribute one ball to each student. Give a tagging implement to about 10 percent of the class. If tagged, a student freezes and then waits to be unfrozen by any other student. Play for 2 to 3 minutes and then switch Its.

⦾ Play Mystery Dribble Tag (see Mystery Tag, found on page 98).

Basketball Knock Away
Ages 8 and up

Everyone dribbles a ball at the same time. The students attempt to keep control of their balls while other students try to cause them to lose control. This game has constant motion and is fantastic dribbling practice.

Topics

⦾ Aerobic endurance

⦾ Manipulative skills

⦾ Cooperation

⦾ Safety awareness

Objectives

⦾ Psychomotor—Dribble a ball with control while changing directions and speed.

⦾ Cognitive—Understand the importance of dribbling a ball while looking at the whole court; understand the game's aerobic fitness benefits.

⦾ Affective—Appreciate the individual differences in ball-handling skills; move safely; cooperate by gently tapping the ball away.

Equipment

⦾ 1 playground ball for each student

⦾ 5 to 8 basketballs

Safety

⦾ Explain that using an up-and-down motion will result in slapping the hand and committing a foul.

⦾ Demonstrate how to tap a ball away using a side-handed motion rather than an up-and-down motion.

⦾ Remind students to move with control.

Game

1. Each student receives one playground ball.

2. Students spread out in scatter formation.

3. The students practice moving while dribbling throughout the play area, without looking directly at the ball.

4. Choose five to eight students to exchange their playground balls for basketballs.

5. On the go signal, the students with basketballs attempt to use their free hands to gently tap the balls away from the students with playground balls.

6. All students continuously dribble.

7. If a student with a playground ball loses control of her ball (either accidentally or because it was tapped away), she freezes. Another student may pick up any loose playground ball and, while holding one playground ball, dribble to a frozen student and hand her the ball. The frozen student may then reenter the game.

8. Play for 2 to 4 minutes and begin again with new students dribbling a basketball.

Variations

- Vary the locomotor skill. Running may be one of the skills, since dribbling a ball naturally slows the students down.

- Students must dribble with the nondominant hand.

- Instead of knocking the ball away, the basketball dribblers may tag the playground ball dribblers. Upon being tagged, students freeze with the ball held in two hands. The frozen students may be unfrozen by any other student who takes the ball from the frozen student, begins dribbling it, and allows the frozen student to take over.

Basketball Shoot and Tag
Ages 8 and up

This basketball game combines shooting and rebounding skills with tag. The game provides students safety from being tagged and also offers them a chance to become risk takers. The constant motion provides a good aerobic workout.

Topics

- Aerobic endurance
- Manipulative skills
- Cooperation

Objectives

◉ Psychomotor—Dribble a basketball with control; shoot a basketball from close range and rebound the ball quickly.

◉ Cognitive—Understand the use of the pads of the fingers for controlled dribbling; understand the reasons for dribbling without looking directly at the ball; understand the aerobic fitness benefits.

◉ Affective—Appreciate individual differences in ability; cooperate to keep the game moving and safe.

Equipment

◉ 1 basketball or playground ball for each student

◉ 3 to 8 foam balls or disks to use as tagging implements

Safety

◉ Move with control.

◉ When taking a shot, make sure not to shoot over the head of someone else. Find a clear path to the basket.

◉ Watch for other rebounding balls.

Game

1. Each student receives one ball.

2. Students spread out in scatter formation.

3. The students practice dribbling throughout general space. Remind the students to keep the head up while dribbling.

4. They may also take one shot at a basket, quickly get the rebound, and move on to a different basket.

5. Encourage the students to shoot from close range.

6. Remove three to eight balls from play. These players receive a foam implement to use as a tagging device. They are the Its for the first round.

7. At the go signal, the students with the basketballs or playground balls dribble and shoot. When they are in control of the ball, they may not be tagged. If they lose control of the ball or take a shot, they may be tagged. Any time a student shoots, that student may be tagged while the ball is not in his hands.

8. If a student is tagged, he freezes without the ball. To unfreeze him, another student retrieves a loose ball and hands it to the frozen student.

9. Students play for 2 to 5 minutes and then change Its.

Variations

- Students may be tagged at any time. Instead of freezing when tagged, they must successfully make a basket from a designated area in order to get back in the game.
- Students total the amount of baskets made after each round and try to beat each previous round. This variation encourages more shot taking.
- Allow only one kind of shot. For example, allow only foul shots.
- Give the Its a basketball. They must dribble the ball while tagging other students.

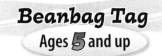

Beanbag Tag
Ages 5 and up

Beanbags can be used for all kinds of balancing and tossing activities. This game keeps the students moving while giving them plenty of practice manipulating a beanbag.

Topics

- Aerobic endurance
- Locomotor skills
- Manipulative skills
- Cooperation

Objectives

- Psychomotor—Demonstrate various locomotor skills while balancing or tossing and catching a beanbag.
- Cognitive—Understand body alignment; know body parts; be able to explain the aerobic benefits of the game; understand the application of force and absorption to successful tossing and catching.
- Affective—Cooperate to keep the game moving and safe.

Equipment

- 1 beanbag for each student
- 1 to 3 foam balls or disks to use as tagging implements

Safety

- Look in the direction you are going.
- Move with control.

Game

1. Each student receives one beanbag.

2. Students spread out in scatter formation.

3. The students move with the beanbags balanced on various body parts. They may also move while tossing and catching their beanbags. If these skills were taught previously, review quickly.

4. Choose one to three students to be the Its. Give the Its a foam ball or disk to use as a tagging implement. Call out a body part. Everyone, including the Its, moves around with a beanbag balanced on that body part. Once movement begins, students may not touch the beanbags with the hands. If a student's beanbag falls, if she touches it with her hands, or if she is tagged, she is frozen with the beanbag on the floor.

5. When tagged, the student lets her beanbag fall to the floor. A frozen student may be freed if another student, without losing control of his own beanbag, bends down, picks up the beanbag on the floor, and replaces it on the frozen student's proper body part. The helping student may not be tagged while he is freeing someone.

6. If there are several Its and one of them drops a beanbag, another It may free the frozen one. After 2 to 4 minutes, choose new Its. If only one It was chosen, the round is over when the It's beanbag falls off. Choose a new It.

Variations

⊚ Vary the locomotor skills.

⊚ Allow the students to hold the beanbag against the body part that was called. This variation may be used at any time to make the game more aerobic.

⊚ The Its do not have beanbags. They must walk. The other students may use any locomotor skill as long as they maintain control of their beanbags.

⊚ Let the students toss and catch their beanbags as they move throughout the play area. In this variation, the Its do not have beanbags. The students are safe as long as they are in control of their beanbags. A student may be tagged if her beanbag hits the floor. She may be freed if another student, while tossing and catching his beanbag, retrieves a loose beanbag and hands it to the frozen student.

⊚ Proceed as usual, except that the Its get one point for every student they tag. No one freezes in this variation, so the game becomes more aerobic.

⊚ No-Touch Tag—This is a progressive tag game. Everyone has a beanbag. The students place the beanbags on their heads. The students move (according to your directions) at various speeds and levels and use locomotor skills. When a beanbag falls, the student places it back in the crate or container. That student may then try to cause other beanbags to fall, without touching anyone, by moving very close to other students, trying to make them laugh, skipping in circles around them, and generally trying to distract those children who still have a beanbag. Students try to be the last one left with a beanbag.

Bowling Pin Tag
Ages 6 and up

Plastic bowling pins are terrific for eye–hand coordination. Students can toss them in a variety of ways, ranging from very easy to very difficult. Bowling Pin Tag combines this unique eye–hand coordination practice with tag. The children also have to make many choices as to how they want to play the game.

Topics

- ⊚ Aerobic endurance
- ⊚ Locomotor skills
- ⊚ Manipulative skills
- ⊚ Cooperation

Objectives

- ⊚ Psychomotor—Demonstrate at least three locomotor skills; demonstrate tossing and catching ability.
- ⊚ Cognitive—Explain the aerobic benefits of the game; understand the importance of watching a piece of equipment into the hands when tossing and catching.
- ⊚ Affective—Cooperate to play the game safely and fairly; appreciate individual differences in tossing and catching ability.

Equipment

- ⊚ 1 or more plastic bowling pins (or empty tennis cans, as substitutes) for every two students
- ⊚ 3 to 10 tagging implements, such as foam Frisbees or balls

Safety

- ⊚ Move with control.
- ⊚ Toss the pins carefully so as not to hit other students.

Game

1. The students place the bowling pins randomly throughout the play area.

2. Students spread out in scatter formation.

3. The students practice two or three locomotor skills, attempting to avoid knocking over the pins. Count negative points for each pin knocked over. Students play a couple of 2-minute practice rounds and see how few negative points they can score. Reset the pins after each round.

4. Choose approximately 10 percent of the class to be the Its. Give each It a tagging implement.

5. At the go signal, with everyone performing the same locomotor skill, the Its attempt to tag the rest of the students. Anyone knocking over a pin must freeze (including the Its) until another student picks up that pin.

6. When a student is tagged, she picks up any pin, tosses and catches it two or more (depending on skill and age) consecutive times, replaces it, and then reenters the game.

7. Students are also safe at any time if they pick up a pin and toss and catch it. However, if the pin drops, they freeze until another student picks up that pin.

8. After 2 to 3 minutes, end the round and choose (or let the students choose) new Its.

Variations

◉ Vary the locomotor skills.

◉ Vary the way the students may reenter the game after they are tagged. For example, they may find another frozen student and toss and catch a pin with that person.

◉ Vary the number of successful consecutive tosses and catches required to unfreeze a student.

◉ During the practice stage of the game, allow the students to toss and catch the pins in a number of ways. Some of these ways include holding the pin by the neck so that the pin spins in the air, holding the pin by the fat part (body) and either spinning it or trying to keep it from spinning, and holding the pin by the bottom (foot), bouncing it off the floor, and then trying to catch it after one bounce.

◉ During the locomotor skills practice, tell the students that if they succeed in not touching any of the pins in 2 minutes, they can proceed to the tag game without any additional practice.

Cranky Crab Tag
Ages 5 and up

This tag game builds muscular strength and endurance. It is also a great game when there is a limited area available. For those times when half of your play area is being used for some other purpose, this game is the perfect choice. Any age can play it, but modify it for younger children by giving them longer rest periods.

Topics

- Muscular strength and endurance
- Locomotor skills
- Cooperation

Objectives

- Psychomotor—Be able to move in a crab position for at least 1 minute and demonstrate the proper push-up position.
- Cognitive—Understand that muscular strength and endurance are acquired by using specific muscles repeatedly (overloading them).
- Affective—Work cooperatively in a large group.

Equipment

1 soft foam disk or ball for every four or five students

Safety

Look in the direction you are going.

Game

1. Students spread out in scatter formation. Have the students practice the crab walk by balancing on their hands and feet with the stomach facing the ceiling (or up).
2. Set boundary lines closer. For example, use only half or a quarter of a gymnasium.
3. Choose four or five students to be the Its.
4. The Its are the cranky crabs. These crabs do not like to see happy crabs moving around, because it disturbs their peace.
5. Give each cranky crab a freeze claw (fleece ball, Nerf ball, or foam disk).
6. The cranky crabs move around and try to tag the rest of the crabs with the piece of equipment called the freeze claw.
7. When the students are tagged, they sit on the floor with their legs straight out and hands on the floor. A frozen crab may get back into the game if a

happy crab comes and places his feet against the feet of the frozen crab and pushes the feet back into a crab position.

8. Play for 1 to 2 minutes and then choose new cranky crabs.

Variations

- Safety tag—Students may rest and not be tagged if they turn over in the push-up position.
- Progressive tag—Begin with one cranky crab and use no equipment. Each crab that is tagged becomes a cranky crab and helps tag the others. In this version, the children who are not It move as if they were a snake, a seal, or any other animal that requires them to use upper-body strength and endurance.
- Tired cranky crabs may rest by sitting down and then rolling or tossing their freeze claw at moving crabs. However, after rolling or tossing their freeze claw, they must move in crab position and retrieve it before tagging anyone else.

Domino Tag
Ages 5 and up

Children love to discover what is in a closed hand. This game gives children of all ages an excellent workout and has them use their cognitive skills to try to acquire the dominoes.

Topics

- Aerobic endurance
- Locomotor skills
- Cooperation
- Safety awareness

Objectives

- Psychomotor—Move safely while demonstrating a variety of locomotor skills.
- Cognitive—Be able to explain the aerobic benefits of the game; understand several kinds of locomotor skills.
- Affective—Cooperate to keep the game moving and safe.

Equipment

5 to 15 dominoes or other small objects

Safety

⚠️ ⊚ Instruct the students to look in the direction they are going and move with control.

⊚ All tags must be light on the shoulder.

Game

1. The students walk throughout the play area with both hands open. Place a domino in some of the open hands and fake placing a domino in the others. Instruct the students to close the hand whether you give them a domino or fake placing one in their hand.

2. After distributing 5 to 15 dominoes, give the signal for the game to begin. Identify a locomotor skill. At the go signal all students, with one hand closed, skip, walk, gallop, slide, and so forth while attempting to tag other students lightly on the shoulder.

3. When a student is tagged, she opens her closed hand. If the hand contains a domino, she gives it to the person who tagged her. After giving up a domino, a student cannot immediately tag that person back. She must first tag at least one other person. Alternatively, instead of the no tagging back rule, each student who loses a domino must spin around two times before tagging anyone else.

4. Simultaneous tags require both students to open their hands and exchange a domino if they have one.

5. If a student acquires several dominoes, she only has to give up a single domino when tagged. All dominoes must be kept in one hand.

6. Play for 2 to 3 minutes. At the stop signal, the students who have the dominoes get one point for each.

7. Collect the dominoes and start again.

Variations

⊚ Vary the locomotor skills.

⊚ The students sit with their eyes closed while you hand out the dominoes.

⊚ Divide the students into four teams. Distribute the dominoes evenly among the teams. The object of the game is for each team to acquire the most dominoes in a given time period.

⊚ Choose 10 percent of the class to be Its. Give each It a tagging implement. The Its try to collect all the dominoes in 2 minutes. When a student is tagged, he stops and opens his hands. If there is a domino in one, he gives it to the tagger.

Endangered Species Tag
Ages 7 and up

I invented this game after conferring with a second-grade teacher. The class was studying endangered species. They came up with an amazing list of animals and had a great time playing the game. You can also change this game to involve any kind of animal or mechanical movement.

Topics

⊚ Aerobic endurance

⊚ Locomotor skills

⊚ Cooperation

⊚ Curriculum integration

⊚ Safety awareness

Objectives

⊚ Psychomotor—Demonstrate the ability to interpret the movements of several types of animals that are considered endangered species.

⊚ Cognitive—Understand what an endangered species is and why animals are endangered; formulate strategies for moving quickly and safely; understand the aerobic benefits of the game.

⊚ Affective—Appreciate individual differences in ability; cooperate to move safely and achieve success as a group.

Equipment

⊚ 4 to 6 soft disks or balls to use as tagging implements

⊚ 1 small ball, such as a tennis ball, for each student

⊚ 2 or 3 hula hoops or boxes

Safety

Instruct the students to move with control and look in the direction they are going.

Game

1. Distribute a tennis ball to each student.

2. Place the hula hoops or boxes in two or three locations in the corners of the playing area.

3. Choose about 10 percent of the class to be the hunters and give each hunter a soft ball or disk to use as a tagging implement.

4. Ask the class to pick an endangered species and then say, "How do you think that animal might move? Can you all move the way that animal does? The hunters are going to try to wipe out this animal by tagging the animal."

5. Students begin the game in scatter formation.

6. The hunters move according to the speed of the endangered species. For slow-moving animals, the hunters may only walk. For faster-moving animals, allow the hunters to skip, gallop, or slide.

7. Upon making a successful tag, the hunter takes the tennis ball (which represents an unborn baby or egg) and brings it to one of the boxes or hoops.

8. The tagged animal freezes and remains frozen until another animal friend can take a ball back from the hoop or box and give it to the frozen animal.

9. Animals may take only one ball at a time.

10. The hunters may work together to try to protect the eggs they acquire.

11. After 3 minutes, if the hunters have not gathered all the eggs, start the game again with new hunters and a new endangered species.

Variations

◎ Allow the hunters a choice of locomotor skills.

◎ Choose two students to be the environmentalists. Their job is to get the balls back to the frozen animals. In this version only the environmentalists can free the animals, and no one may stop them from taking the tennis balls from the box or hoop.

◎ Divide the class into four teams. Each team represents an endangered species. The object of the game is to be the team with the most tennis balls left at the end of 3 minutes. All the other rules apply.

◎ Increase the number of hunters until the animals have very little chance of survival. Discuss the results with the students.

◎ Keep the hunters at 10 percent of the class but allow them to move faster than the animals. Discuss the results with the students.

Gymnastic Tag
Ages 8 and up

This game combines gymnastic skills with tag. It allows the children to practice gymnastic skills while participating in a game situation. Children choose how much time they wish to spend on gymnastics as opposed to how much time they want to be involved in the tag game.

Topics

- ⑥ Aerobic endurance
- ⑥ Muscular strength and endurance
- ⑥ Tumbling skills
- ⑥ Cooperation
- ⑥ Safety awareness

Objectives

- ⑥ Psychomotor—Demonstrate at least three tumbling skills.
- ⑥ Cognitive—Understand the importance of transferring body weight in order to be successful at tumbling; describe the aerobic nature of the game.
- ⑥ Affective—Appreciate individual differences in ability; cooperate to keep the game moving and safe.

Equipment

- ⑥ 6 to 8 mats
- ⑥ 5 gym scooters
- ⑥ 5 tagging implements (foam Frisbees or balls)
- ⑥ Music (optional)

Safety

- ⑥ Look in the direction you are going.
- ⑥ Make sure there is no one on the mat before attempting a gymnastic skill.
- ⑥ Move with control.
- ⑥ Practice only gymnastic skills that you have been taught and that you have done successfully without a spotter.

Game

1. After the students have received some basic training in tumbling skills, they may then choose to demonstrate these skills during this game.
2. The students begin by choosing one of the available mats and forming a line behind it. For safety reasons, they must perform all tumbling skills in the same direction.
3. After the students have chosen a mat, select 10 percent of the class to become the first Its. These students each sit on a gym scooter and receive a tagging implement (see figure 4.1).

4. Students may not be tagged as long as they are in line at a mat, performing a tumbling skill, or just exiting a mat (allow the students three steps in any direction upon their leaving a mat).

5. As soon as they leave a line or take more than three steps off a mat, students may be tagged.

6. Place one light mat in the center of the playing area (this mat is used only to free students who are tagged).

7. When a student is tagged, she freezes with feet together and hands above the head. The frozen student may be freed if another student drags the light mat over to her. After performing a tumbling skill, she looks for another frozen student to free. If there are no frozen students, the mat is left alone.

8. Students may not be tagged while dragging this mat.

9. Play each round for 2 to 3 minutes. Start over with new students as Its.

10. Use lively music to start and stop each round.

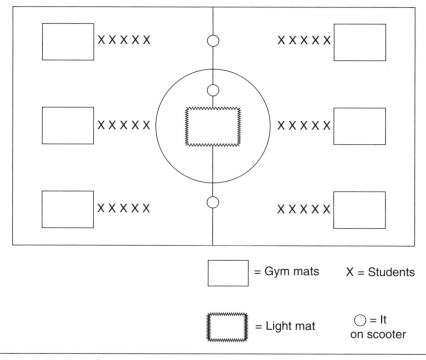

Figure 4.1   Floor diagram for Gymnastic Tag.

Variations

⊚ Specify one tumbling skill to demonstrate but allow students who cannot perform that skill to choose an alternate.

⊚ Vary the number of Its or mats.

⊚ Instead of using gym scooters, the Its move using a designated locomotor skill.

Hoop Tag
Ages 7 and up

Hoop Tag is a form of safety tag because it allows children the opportunity to safely rest. The children like the mental challenge of deciding when it is safe to move and when it is safe to help others. However, safety tag diminishes the aerobic benefits of the game. This factor gives you a good chance to discuss what makes one game or activity more aerobic than another.

Topics

⊚ Aerobic endurance

⊚ Locomotor skills

⊚ Manipulative skills

⊚ Cooperation

⊚ Safety awareness

Objectives

⊚ Psychomotor—Move safely and carefully while running, skipping, galloping, or walking.

⊚ Cognitive—Understand and explain the aerobic benefits of the game.

⊚ Affective—Cooperate to achieve the common goal of keeping the game moving and safe.

Equipment

⊚ 1 hoop for each student or 1 hoop for every two students

⊚ 3 or 4 soft objects to be used as tagging tools (foam Frisbees or foam balls)

Safety

⚠
- ⓖ Avoid collisions.
- ⓖ Move with control.
- ⓖ Pick up and place hoops carefully so as not to hit anyone with the hoop.
- ⓖ Look in the direction you are going.

Game

1. Distribute the hoops to either half or all of the students.
2. Students scatter the hoops throughout the play area.
3. All students then practice moving throughout the play area employing various locomotor skills, while trying not to touch any of the hoops. However, a student may rest at any time by standing inside a hoop.
4. After one or two practice rounds, which should last 1 to 2 minutes each, take away any hoop that students touch or assign one or two students to take away the touched hoops.
5. After two or three rounds of general movement, choose three or four students to be It and give each It a foam tagging tool.
6. Students begin the game in scatter formation.
7. Choose a locomotor skill for students to use.
8. At the go signal, the Its try to tag as many students as possible. When students are tagged, they freeze with feet together and hands together above the head. A frozen student may be freed if another student picks up any unoccupied hoop and places it over the frozen student, letting it fall to the floor.
9. Once inside the hoop, the student may return to the game.
10. Any student is safe while standing inside a hoop. However, when a student picks up a hoop, he may be tagged at any time. The students can never be safe while holding a hoop (this rule discourages students from running around with a hoop in their hands). Nor can a student be safe by standing inside the hoop he picked up. If a student picks up a hoop, it cannot be the one he stands in to be safe; he must drop it and find a different one.
11. If tagged when holding a hoop, a student freezes and places the hoop on the floor beside him.
12. Play for a designated time period and then choose new Its.

Variations

- ⓖ Vary the locomotor skills.
- ⓖ Choose one student to time each round. Place a crate of balls next to that student and have her toss all the balls, one at a time, into an empty crate. When she has transferred all the balls, the round is over.

Monster Tag
Ages 5 to 7

You may use this Halloween game at any time of the year by substituting any-thing else for the monster. For example, play Machine Tag—each child chooses a machine's movement to interpret.

Topics

- Aerobic endurance
- Locomotor skills
- Cooperation
- Safety awareness

Objectives

- Psychomotor—Perform a variety of locomotor skills.
- Cognitive—Understand that there are various ways of interpreting move-ment.
- Affective—Move safely and cooperate to achieve success as a group.

Equipment

None

Safety

- Move with control.
- Look in the direction you are going.

Game

1. Choose one student to be It.
2. Say, "You are all in a haunted house. You cannot get out of the house. All the windows are sealed, and the doors are locked. There is a monster in the house that is trying to find you. If the monster finds you, you turn into this monster and you must help the monster find everyone else."
3. Choose a locomotor skill. All the students move by skipping, galloping, walking, or doing whatever skill you choose. The student who is selected to be It chooses a kind of monster and interprets the way this particular monster moves.
4. When a human is tagged, that person must move in the same way as the original monster. The game continues until all but one human is caught. That human becomes the new monster.

Variations

- The game continues until everyone is caught. Pick a new monster.
- One human chases the monsters. The monsters change back into humans when they are tagged. The human chooses any locomotor skill except running.
- Monsters link elbows and move as one, or they may break off into smaller groups.
- Choose three to five students to become a certain kind of monster. When the monsters tag a human, that human must freeze. Choose a way for the humans to unfreeze each other. For example, two students link arms around the frozen human and chant, "One, two, three, human free."
- Hold up signs with the names of various kinds of monsters. The monsters interpret the way that particular monster moves. Change signs often.

Moving Duck Duck Goose
Ages 5 to 10

Moving Duck Duck Goose solves the problem of only two children moving at once, as in the usual version of the game. In this version, every child is moving at the same time.

Topics

- Aerobic endurance
- Locomotor skills
- Cooperation
- Safety awareness

Objectives

- Psychomotor—Move safely while skipping, walking, galloping, or jogging in an attempt to tag or avoid being tagged by another student.
- Cognitive—Understand that exercise increases the heart rate.
- Affective—Cooperate to involve all children and achieve a common goal of keeping the game moving and safe.

Equipment

5 to 10 soft balls or other objects that can be used as tagging implements

Safety

Remind students to look in the direction they are going and to move with control.

Game

Before playing this game for the first time, ask the children how many know how to play Duck Duck Goose. Briefly discuss the game and explain why it does not really belong in your curriculum (only two children moving while the rest are sitting or cheering, no attempt to improve spatial awareness, and no skills practice). This would also be a good time to discuss the difference between an educational game and a recreational game.

1. Choose 10 to 20 percent of the class to be Its.
2. Give each It a soft foam or fleece ball to use as a tagging tool.
3. Students spread out in scatter formation.
4. The rest of the class skips or gallops throughout the play area. The students who are Its walk and touch the skipping players with the tagging tool while chanting, "Duck, duck, duck," and so forth.
5. When an It touches a player and says, "Goose," the It quickly gives that student the tagging tool and skips or gallops away.
6. The goose skips or gallops after the It who just gave him the ball (tagging tool).
7. When the goose makes the tag, he then becomes a new It and begins to walk around the gymnasium while chanting, "Duck, duck, duck," and so forth. If the goose cannot catch the It, he may drop the tagging tool on the floor. Anyone else may pick it up and become a new It.

Variations

⊙ Change the locomotor skill. The Its may move the same way as the rest of the class.

⊙ Instead of giving the tagging tool, the It may drop it at the feet of the goose.

⊙ Vary the number of Its.

⊙ Time each round for 1 to 2 minutes. After each round ask the students who are currently Its to choose someone to replace them.

Mystery Tag
Ages 5 and up

Everyone loves a mystery. This tag game is great fun because no one knows who, if anyone, has chosen her. Tell the children to try to sneak up on their mystery persons and tag them lightly on the shoulder. Additionally, students may play this game instead of any other type of tag game that uses manipulative equipment.

Topics

- Aerobic endurance
- Locomotor skills
- Manipulative skills
- Cooperation
- Safety awareness

Objectives

- Psychomotor—Move safely while demonstrating several locomotor and manipulative skills.
- Cognitive—Understand and be able to explain the aerobic benefits of the game.
- Affective—Cooperate to achieve the common goal of keeping the game moving and safe.

Equipment

None, or any kind of manipulative

Safety

Tag lightly and move with control.

Game

1. Explain that each player secretly chooses one student to tag. Since no one knows who is trying to tag him or how many people are trying to tag him, the game is called Mystery Tag.

2. Encourage the students to choose someone who is standing or sitting on the other side of the play area.

3. The students place their hands on their heads when they have chosen their mystery student.

4. Students spread out in scatter formation.

5. On the go signal, the students attempt to tag the one person they secretly chose. Upon being tagged, that student is frozen in place. She may be unfrozen by any student who greets her and says, "You're a nice person, I like you, you're free."

6. After about 1 to 2 minutes, students stop the action and choose a new secret person. Students may not choose someone they have already tagged. To make sure the children understand the concept of only tagging the person they originally chose, after the first round is over, ask any students who were tagged by two or more people to stand. Ask them who tagged them. Then ask whether those children tagged anyone else. Sometimes the first time you play this game, children will tag more than one person.

Variations

◉ Change locomotor skills.

◉ Change the number of students each person can tag. Here's an example: "This time can you choose three other students that you would like to tag?"

◉ Change the way in which the students are freed: shaking hands with the frozen student, linking elbows, passing between open legs, giving a shoulder massage, or any other way you choose.

◉ Give each student a beanbag and require them to balance the beanbag on a body part while moving throughout the play area.

◉ Instead of tagging the secret person, students link elbows with the secret person and move on to try to link elbows with other secret partners.

◉ Use another kind of manipulative. For example, students may dribble a playground ball while moving. When someone tags them, they freeze, place the ball between the feet, and wait for someone else to pick up the ball and hand it to them.

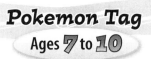

Pokemon Tag
Ages 7 to 10

This tag game is based on the popular toy, Pokemon. However, students can play the game as another form of tag by simply changing the name of the game and the name of the equipment. One of the benefits of this game is the decision-making process students must use to figure out how and when to help each other.

Topics

⊚ Aerobic endurance

⊚ Locomotor skills

⊚ Cooperation

Objectives

⊚ Psychomotor—Demonstrate at least two locomotor skills.

⊚ Cognitive—Understand the cardiovascular nature of the game; develop a strategy for success.

⊚ Affective—Appreciate individual differences in ability; cooperate to make the game successful.

Equipment

⊚ 4 soft foam balls

⊚ 4 hoops

⊚ 3 tennis balls per student

Safety

⚠ Remind students to move with control and look in the direction they are going.

Game

1. Place one hoop in each corner of the play area. Each hoop represents a Pokemon trainer's home.

2. Choose four trainers.

3. Give one soft foam ball to each trainer. These foam balls are the Pokeballs.

4. The trainers take the Pokeballs to their homes.

5. Give the rest of the class three tennis balls each. These balls represent the Pokemon.

6. Students spread out in scatter formation.

7. On the go signal, everyone skips, walks, or gallops. The trainers attempt to tag anyone holding a Pokemon. They use the Pokeball as the tagging implement. After a successful tag, the trainer takes one Pokemon (tennis ball). The trainer immediately takes that Pokemon back to his home and places it securely in the hoop.

8. The trainer may then go out and try to get more Pokemon.

9. If a Pokemon drops, any student may pick it up. However, no student may ever have more than three Pokemon.

10. Any student who loses all three Pokemon must freeze, but she can get back in the game if someone else gives her a Pokemon.

11. It might be necessary to discuss the advantages of giving up a Pokemon to a frozen student (helping others, more people in the game so less of a chance of being tagged).

12. Play each round for 2 to 3 minutes. Give the stop signal. The trainers go back to their homes. The rest of the students walk slowly around the play area until their heart rates slow down. They then sit. The trainers count their Pokemon. The trainer with the most Pokemon becomes the Pokemon Master for that round.

13. Pick four new trainers. Allow the other students to go to the corner hoops and retrieve three Pokemon to begin a new round.

Variations

◉ Allow trainers to collect more than one Pokemon at a time. However, the trainer may not take more than one from each person.

◉ Allow only one style of locomotor movement.

◉ Allow trainers to battle. If a trainer has a Pokemon in his hand, another trainer may tag him. Do not allow tag backs.

◉ Change the name to Superman Tag or any other variation, such as Supergirl Tag, Super Tag, or even Kryptonite Tag. In this version the trainers are Superman. The balls that Superman carries are kryptonite balls. The tennis balls represent lead, which may be used to encase the kryptonite. The more lead the Supermen collect, the better they do in the round.

◉ Make up your own story from a popular book, TV show, or movie.

Quest for Freedom Tag
Ages 8 and up

On first reading, this game appears complicated. However, it is quite easy to learn and gives the students a chance to think and practice their manipulative skills while playing an exciting game. Tell the students that their task is to remain free for as long as possible. If tagged by a restrictor, they must tag that restrictor back to regain their freedom. When explaining the game, remind the students that only the restrictors can get a ball from the side. Everyone else must tag the restrictor back in order to get a ball.

Topics

⊚ Aerobic endurance

⊚ Locomotor skills

⊚ Manipulative skills

⊚ Cooperation

⊚ Safety awareness

Objectives

⊚ Psychomotor—Demonstrate several locomotor skills; dribble a basketball, playground ball, or soccer ball with control.

⊚ Cognitive—Understand the aerobic benefits of the game; understand the amount of force necessary to control a ball; understand the strategy involved in playing the game.

⊚ Affective—Work cooperatively to make the game successful and safe.

Equipment

⊚ 4 or 5 foam balls or disks, to be used only by restrictors

⊚ 2 or 3 balls that are not playground balls, basketballs, or soccer balls (for the freedom ball keepers)

⊚ Enough playground balls, basketballs, or soccer balls for each student

Safety

Remind the students to look in the direction they are going and to move with control.

Game

1. Place the soccer, playground, and basketballs in several locations on the perimeter of the play area. Use several bags, containers, or racks to hold the balls.

2. Choose four or five students to be It. The Its will be known as the restrictors. Discuss the meaning of the word.

3. Choose two or three students to be freedom ball keepers. Give them a special kind of ball to throw. Freedom ball keepers cannot be tagged.

4. Place the restrictors on a line in front of the play area. The other students are in scatter formation.

5. Choose a locomotor skill. Do not allow running except when manipulating a ball.

6. On the go signal the restrictors attempt to tag students, using the foam disk or foam ball as the tagging tool.

7. The restrictor hands the tagged student the foam disk. That student freezes while holding the disk. After handing off the disk, the restrictor goes to the side and chooses a ball. The restrictor manipulates this ball while looking out for the student she just tagged.

8. The freedom ball keepers find the frozen students. They toss or throw the freedom ball to the frozen student, who catches the ball on the fly and tosses or throws it back to the freedom ball keeper. If the frozen student misses the ball, the freedom ball keeper may try again or move on to another frozen student. The throwing distance may be prearranged or may be chosen by the freedom ball keeper.

9. When the frozen student is freed, he attempts to tag the restrictor who froze him. Remind students to use the designated locomotor skill.

10. When he tags that restrictor, the unfrozen student returns the disk to her and takes the ball from her.

11. That student is now free to practice dribbling the ball without worrying about being tagged.

12. The restrictor looks for another student without a ball to tag.

13. The goal of the game is to be one of the last few students in each round without a ball.

14. After most of the students have a ball, stop play and choose new students to be the restrictors and the freedom ball keepers.

Note: Some children may try to be tagged on purpose so that they can play with a ball. Emphasize that allowing oneself to be tagged on purpose goes against the nature of the game and is a form of cheating.

Variations

⊚ Vary the locomotor skills.

⊚ Vary the kinds of balls in use.

⊚ Vary the manipulative skills.

⊚ The game can be made more complicated by allowing the students who have achieved freedom and are dribbling the various kinds of balls to tag each other. In this version, a tagged student freezes but gets back into the game if someone else tags the person who tagged the frozen student.

Secret Santa Tag
Ages 6 and up

This game was created for the holidays but can be played anytime by making a simple name change. For example, you can call the game Find Your Secret Friend Tag. It is similar to Mystery Tag, except that the children are not given a choice of whom to tag. You can combine this game with manipulative skills by adding equipment.

Topics

- Aerobic endurance
- Locomotor skills
- Safety awareness
- Holiday activities

Objectives

- Psychomotor—Combine five locomotor skills in a tag game.
- Cognitive—Understand how to move safely while dodging other students; understand the cardiovascular benefits of the game.
- Affective—Be able to follow simple rules to keep the game moving and safe.

Equipment

2 index cards for each student

Safety

Remind students to look in the direction they are going, tag lightly, and move with control.

Game

1. Each student writes her name on two index cards.
2. Collect the cards.
3. Each student receives one card.
4. The rest of the cards go in a pile or in a box.
5. Show the class how to perform an easy dance step (optional).
6. Students spread out in scatter formation.
7. Choose a locomotor skill.

8. Each student reads the name on his index card; he is that person's Secret Santa. If a student chooses his own name, he returns the card to the pile and chooses another one.

9. On the go signal, students attempt to tag their Secret Santa. Upon tagging their Santa, students show the card to that person, return the card to the pile, and choose another card.

10. When a Secret Santa is tagged, she goes to the North Pole (a designated place in the play area), performs the Secret Santa dance step (any easy combination of steps), and then returns to the game.

11. Each round is about 3 minutes long. The students see how many Secret Santas they can tag within the 3 minutes and try to beat this number in the next round.

12. After each round, change the locomotor skill or discuss ways to improve the game.

Variations

⊚ Vary the locomotor skills.

⊚ Vary the kind of activities the tagged Santa performs.

⊚ The tagged Santa freezes, to be unfrozen by another student. Use various ways to unfreeze. For example, the person freeing the frozen student sings a chorus of "Jingle Bells."

⊚ Give two cards to each student. The student tags both Secret Santas before returning the cards to the pile.

⊚ Add any kind of manipulative equipment, such as basketballs.

Soccer Tag
Ages 7 and up

This tag game provides controlled soccer dribbling practice by allowing the soccer players to free the frozen students. The soccer players do not have to worry about being tagged or about tagging other students.

Topics

⊚ Aerobic endurance

⊚ Manipulative skills

⊚ Cooperation

Objectives

⚙ Psychomotor—Demonstrate how to dribble a soccer ball while moving and changing direction quickly.

⚙ Cognitive—Understand the application of force needed to control a soccer ball; be able to explain the aerobic benefits of the game.

⚙ Affective—Work cooperatively to keep the game moving.

Equipment

⚙ Soccer balls or playground balls for 30 to 90 percent of the class

⚙ Foam balls for 10 to 30 percent of the class.

Safety

⚙ Move with control.

⚙ Look in the direction you are going.

Game

1. Divide the class into thirds.

2. One-third of the class are the Its, one-third of the class try to avoid the Its, and one-third of the class are soccer players.

3. Each It has a tagging implement such as a foam or Nerf ball. If this equipment is not available, use pinnies or some other identification for the Its. In this case the Its tag lightly on the shoulder, using either hand.

4. Students spread out in scatter formation.

5. The Its skip throughout the play area while attempting to tag the students who do not have soccer balls. The fleeing students also skip.

6. When a student is tagged, he freezes with his legs apart. The soccer players dribble throughout the play area looking for frozen students. A soccer player frees frozen students by dribbling the ball between their open legs.

7. Time each round for 1 to 3 minutes and then switch assignments.

Variations

⚙ Give approximately 90 percent of the students a soccer or playground ball. Give approximately 10 percent of the students a foam ball. The soccer players are safe as long as they are dribbling a ball. However, if they lose control of the ball or stop and rest, they may be tagged. They remain frozen until another soccer player retrieves a loose soccer ball, picks it up, and returns the ball to the frozen player, while still dribbling her own ball.

⚙ Proceed as in the first variation, except that soccer players are given one or more jobs: giving other soccer players a high five, shaking hands with other soccer players, trying to knock the ball away from other soccer players, and so forth.

Sports Tag
Ages 8 and up

Soccer and basketball dribbling skills are combined into a fast-paced game that gives a lot of skills practice, along with a cardiovascular workout.

Topics

- ◎ Aerobic endurance
- ◎ Locomotor skills
- ◎ Manipulative skills
- ◎ Cooperation

Objectives

- ◎ Psychomotor—Be able to dribble a basketball or soccer ball with control while changing speed and direction.
- ◎ Cognitive—Understand the importance of controlling a ball without looking directly at it; understand the game's aerobic benefits.
- ◎ Affective—Appreciate individual differences in ball-handling ability; cooperate to move safely and to achieve success as a group.

Equipment

1 ball for each student, using a variety of balls like basketballs, soccer balls, and playground balls

Safety

- ◎ Move with control.
- ◎ Look in the direction you are going.

Game

1. Distribute a variety of balls to the class.
2. Students practice dribbling their own balls with control.
3. Students may use the playground balls as basketballs or soccer balls.
4. At a given signal (whistle, music stoppage, drumbeat), each student exchanges balls with someone else.
5. After a few minutes of practice and a number of ball exchanges, give a foam ball or foam Frisbee to 10 percent of the students. These students may tag other students with the foam implements as long as they are in control of their own ball.
6. If a basketball player is tagged, he places the ball between his feet. Another player may unfreeze him by picking up the ball and handing it back.

7. If a soccer player is frozen, that player picks up the ball and holds it above her head. Another player may unfreeze this player by taking the ball and placing it down at her feet.

8. If a player is tagged while not in control of a ball, he freezes until another player picks up a loose ball and brings it back to him.

9. After 2 or 3 minutes, the students exchange balls with someone else and redistribute the foam implements.

Variations

⊚ Vary the kinds of balls used.

⊚ Vary the methods of freezing or unfreezing.

⊚ Divide the class into groups of three. Give a different kind of ball to each player in the group. One player in each group is It. The It may tag only the other two players in the group. Here are two options: The round lasts for 1 minute and a tagged player may not be unfrozen; the round lasts for 2 to 3 minutes and a tagged player may be unfrozen by anyone.

Thanksgiving Feast
Ages 7 and up

Holidays create many opportunities to play theme-based games. However, you can revise the game for any occasion by making up various kinds of index cards.

Topics

⊚ Aerobic endurance

⊚ Locomotor skills

⊚ Communication skills

⊚ Collaborative skills

⊚ Reading

Objectives

⊚ Psychomotor—Demonstrate several locomotor skills while dodging and tagging others.

⊚ Cognitive—Read Thanksgiving-related words; understand how to move safely; understand the aerobic benefits of the game.

⊚ Affective—Be willing to work with many different people; communicate as a leader or follower.

//Equipment////////

- ◎ 1 index card for each participant, with a word or picture on it
- ◎ 1 hoop or box for each group of students

//Safety////////

- ◎ Always look in the direction you are going.
- ◎ Move with control.

//Game////////

1. The class divides into five or six equal or almost equal groups. Give each group a list of items to gather for a Thanksgiving feast.

2. Give each group a hoop or box to act as a container for the feast. Scatter the containers on the outside of the playing areas (see figure 4.2).

3. Each group collects one category of items. For example, one group gets the main course, which may include turkey, stuffing, corn, potatoes, vegetables, bread, and cranberry sauce. Other categories may include snacks and drinks, desserts, utensils, relatives, and so forth.

4. Place each item from the lists on individual index cards. For older students, the written word will suffice. You may also cut out matching pictures and place them on the cards. If the class is too young to read, do not hand out lists of items. Give each group pictures of the items it needs.

5. Give each student one index card with the written word on it, a picture, or both. If the card matches the category that the student's group has, she may place that card in her group's hoop or box.

6. Students spread out in scatter formation.

7. Students must make sure they know who is in their group.

8. On the go signal, the students attempt to tag any other student not in their group. They may choose any locomotor skill except running. When one student tags another, they exchange cards. If one student does not have a card, she does not have to exchange; she simply takes a card. If students accidentally tag someone in their group, they must exchange a card or take a card. If the tagged student has more than one card, the tagger only gets the top card. If a card matches a student's category, he attempts to place it into his group's container before being tagged by someone else. Students may not be tagged while they are exchanging cards. Students see which group gathers all its items first.

9. Time the activity and challenge the students to do better after each round.

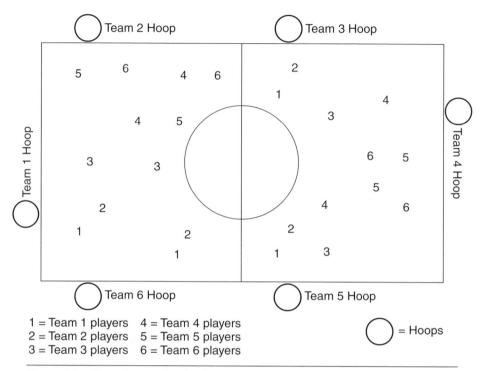

Figure 4.2   Floor diagram for Thanksgiving Feast.

Variations

◎ Cooperative Feast—The students take their cards that do not match their group's category and exchange them with cards that other groups have. Students have to find the cards that they require by asking students in other groups if they have a needed card. The children should give up any card they do not need. The students see how quickly they can exchange their unneeded cards for needed ones and gather the items for the feast. Students not in possession of a card may still ask another student for a card that matches their group's list.

◎ Partner Feast

◎ Competitive—Two or three partners gather behind a traffic cone or line. The index cards are placed facedown in the play area. One partner at a time comes out and searches for a specific category of cards. If they find one, they bring it back to their group and give a high five, and the next person goes. If they turn over a card and it does not match their group's category, they do three jumping jacks or any other quick exercise and quickly return to their group to tag the next person. Students see which group gathers all the cards first. As soon as one group collects all of its cards, the groups change categories and play again.

⊚ Cooperative—This version uses the same rules as the competitive one, but instead of the round ending when one group completes its category, the finished group helps other groups gather their feasts. Time the round and see whether the class can beat its best time.

Turkey Tag
Ages 5 and up

Turkey Tag is another Thanksgiving game that may be played at any time by simply changing the name. This game combines tag with some elementary gymnastic or dance skills.

Topics

⊚ Aerobic endurance

⊚ Locomotor skills

⊚ Manipulative skills

⊚ Aerobic endurance

⊚ Cooperation

⊚ Safety awareness

Objectives

⊚ Psychomotor—Demonstrate the ability to interpret how a turkey moves; accurately roll a soft-type ball.

⊚ Cognitive—Be able to explain the aerobic benefits of the game.

⊚ Affective—Cooperate to keep the game moving and safe.

Equipment

⊚ 3 to 5 foam, Gator Skin, or other soft-type balls

⊚ 3 or 4 mats

 Safety

Remind students to look in the direction they are going and to move with control.

Game

1. Explain that there are three to five hunters (depending on the size of the class) searching for wild turkeys. Hunters represent approximately 15 percent of the class.

2. Give each hunter a soft implement. This implement is the hunter's weapon.

The rest of the students are turkeys. They interpret the way a turkey moves, or they may do a turkey trot (no running).

3. Hunters may not run. They attempt to sneak up on a turkey (walking only) and roll the ball, attempting to hit the turkey on the foot. When a turkey is hit, she freezes with elbows (wings) out. Another turkey locks elbows with the frozen turkey and takes her to the oven. A turkey may not be hunted when helping a frozen turkey.

4. Place a few mats around the outside of the playing area. The mats represent the ovens. The turkeys roll across the mats (log roll, forward roll, and so forth). When they get to the other side, they may get back in the game as newborn turkeys.

5. After 2 to 3 minutes, change hunters.

Variations

⊚ Play square dance music. The turkeys and hunters move by using various square dance steps.

⊚ When hit, the turkeys freeze with elbows out as pretend wings. They may be unfrozen if another turkey links elbows and swings them around three times.

⊚ Instead of throwing the ball, students use it as a tagging implement. In this variation, the hunters may skip or gallop.

⊚ Play progressive tag. Start with one hunter. Do not use any equipment. When a turkey is tagged, the turkey becomes a hunter. The game continues until all the turkeys become hunters.

CHAPTER 5

Fitness Games With a Skill Emphasis

The games in this chapter focus on the psychomotor, cognitive, and affective skills necessary for participating in team and individual sports. Many of the games have multiple uses; by simply changing equipment, you can adapt them to several sports. Each game includes elements of health-related or skill-related fitness. During the explanation, encourage students to explain how to derive maximum fitness from playing the game. After they play, ask the students to describe ways of changing the game to increase psychomotor and socialization skills as well as fitness benefits.

1-2-3 Ball
Ages 8 and up

1-2-3 Ball enables you to work on any sport that involves offensive and defensive skills. This game allows you and the class to be creative and invent rules and activities that promote the skills necessary for playing a particular sport. The game's constant motion provides practice at game speeds while promoting aerobic fitness.

Topics

- Aerobic endurance
- Manipulative skills
- Cooperation

Objectives

- Psychomotor—Demonstrate the ability to perform motor skills necessary to participate in a game or sport.
- Cognitive—Understand the importance of cooperating as a team to produce superior results; be able to explain the aerobic benefits of the game.
- Affective—Appreciate individual differences in ability; enjoy a sport or game for fun rather than for competition.

Equipment

Various, depending on the sport

Safety

- Move with control and control equipment.
- Watch for boundary lines.

Game

1. Choose a sport.
2. The class divides into teams of five to seven players.
3. Play two or three minigames at the same time. Use the width of the gym or play area and divide the area with boundary markers or lines.
4. Designate one team in each minigame as the offense and the other team as the defense.
5. The object of the game is for the offense to reach a predetermined number of points. Only the offense may score points. They may score them in any

way deemed appropriate by you or by class consensus. However, emphasize teamwork, skill, and cooperation. For example, if the game chosen is basketball, one team plays offense until they score 12 points or some other designated total. The team scores 1 point for a contested shot, 2 points for an uncontested shot, and 3 points if an assist is made.

6. If the offense does not score and the defense gets the ball, the defense returns the ball to the offense and play begins again. When the offense reaches 12 points, the teams switch roles.

Variations

⊚ Vary the way points are awarded. For example, in the above basketball game, award a bonus point if all offensive players touch the ball before a basket is made.

⊚ Play for a given amount of time instead of a total number of points. In the competitive version, the team that scores the most points in the designated amount of time is the winner.

⊚ Award points for the defense. For example, in the game of basketball, award 1 point for every defensive rebound, 2 points for an intercepted pass, and 3 points for a clean steal (no foul).

⊚ Use this game for individual sports such as tennis. For example, score 3 points for an ace or winner, 2 points for a forced error, and 1 point for an unforced error.

⊚ Change the amount of equipment; for example, use two basketballs instead of one.

America Online Ball
Ages 8 and up

When signing up for America Online on the computer, one must choose a permanent screen name. This name may never be changed. When you and a partner are playing America Online Ball and choose a way to pass a ball, it becomes your personal screen name.

Topics

⊚ Aerobic endurance

⊚ Manipulative skills

⊚ Cooperation

Objectives

- Psychomotor—Show many ways of manipulating an identical piece of equipment; be able to move while controlling a piece of equipment.
- Cognitive—Understand how much force to use when passing a piece of equipment; understand the aerobic nature of the game.
- Affective—Appreciate differences in manipulative ability; cooperate to keep the game moving and safe.

Equipment

1 tennis ball or other manipulative for each student

Safety

- Move with control.
- Look in the direction you are going.
- Pass equipment carefully.

Game

1. Each student receives one ball.
2. Students divide into pairs. A leftover student can go into one group of three.
3. Use the entire play area.
4. Each pair develops a unique way to pass and move with their pieces of equipment. The partners may use one piece of equipment or both. The way they choose to pass and move becomes their unique screen name.
5. After practicing for a few minutes, students switch partners.
6. The new partners teach their screen names (unique moves) to each other.
7. Students keep switching partners.

Variations

- Vary the equipment.
- Instead of allowing the children to choose to use one or two pieces of equipment, allow them to use only one piece. This variation will be easier for many of the students to perform.
- Ask the students to develop ways to keep the game aerobic. This variation requires the children to move continuously while passing the ball.

Basketball Around the World
Ages 8 and up

Students love to shoot a basketball. This game will have them shooting and passing while in constant motion.

Topics

- Aerobic endurance
- Manipulative skills
- Cooperation

Objectives

- Psychomotor—Demonstrate various types of basketball passes; show proper shooting technique from close range.
- Cognitive—Understand why accurate passing is important; judge the amount of force necessary to shoot from a short distance; understand the aerobic nature of the game.
- Affective—Cooperate with a small group to achieve a group goal; appreciate individual differences in ability.

Equipment

- 1 basketball for every four to six students
- 3 to 6 baskets to shoot at (which can be hoops hung on the wall as makeshift baskets)

Safety

- Move with control.
- Control the speed of passes so as not to hurt others with the ball.

Game

1. The class divides into groups of four to six students.
2. Each group receives one basketball. The object of the game is for each group to score as many points as possible by moving from one basket to another.
3. One person from each group begins by dribbling the ball to one of the baskets. The rest of the group follows. Upon reaching the basket, the ball

is passed to each member of the group. The person who dribbled the ball receives the last pass and attempts a shot at the basket. She may continue to shoot until she scores a basket or she may pass the ball to another member of the group to shoot.

4. After one basket is scored, another member of the group dribbles to the next basket.

5. Play continues until every member of the group has had at least one chance to dribble and shoot, but it may continue for a longer period of time.

6. Players score one point for each basket.

Variations

⊚ Vary the type of pass or allow the students to choose their own passes.

⊚ Allow a limited number of shots at each basket.

⊚ Station one defender at each basket. If the defender touches the ball, the group must move on to another basket.

⊚ Allow one point for hitting the backboard, two points for hitting the rim, and three points for scoring a basket.

⊚ Cooperative—Total all the points at the end of a round. Play again. See whether the class can beat its best score.

⊚ Competitive—See which group scores the most points.

Basketball Concentration
Ages 8 and up

This is a fun guessing game that will have the students moving and practicing all their manipulative basketball skills.

Topics

⊚ Aerobic endurance

⊚ Manipulative skills

⊚ Safety awareness

⊚ Visual discrimination

Objectives

⊚ Psychomotor—Move with a basketball using several dribbling techniques.

⊚ Cognitive—Understand why and when to use various dribbling techniques; be able to explain the aerobic nature of the game.

⊚ Affective—Appreciate differences in ball control ability; cooperate to keep the game safe.

Equipment

1 basketball or playground ball for each student

Safety

⚠ ⊚ Look in the direction you are going.

⊚ Move with control.

Game

1. Each student receives one ball.

2. The students dribble the balls throughout general space.

3. Choose one student to hide his eyes and one or more other students to do something different from the rest of the group. Quickly demonstrate what most of the students will be doing and what one or two students will be doing. Choose the one or two different students by asking for volunteers.

4. The student who hides his eyes attempts to identify the students who are performing something different. He tries to explain what the difference is and why this technique is used (if applicable).

5. For lower grades, keep the skills simple.

The following are suggestions for the game:

⊚ Students dribble with the right hand; one student uses the left.

⊚ Students dribble by alternating one right-handed dribble with one left-handed; one student uses only one hand.

⊚ Students gallop while dribbling; one student skips.

⊚ Students move in a curved path; one student moves in a straight line.

⊚ Students dribble behind their backs; one student dribbles between the legs.

⊚ Students move backward while dribbling; one student moves sideways.

⊚ Students dribble while circling to the left; one student circles to the right.

⊚ Students shake hands with other students while dribbling; one student never shakes hands.

⊚ Students dribble the ball at a moderate rhythm; one student dribbles at a fast or slow rhythm.

⊚ Students use a crossover dribble every time they get to a painted line; one student uses a crossover dribble away from all lines.

Variations

@ Students divide into pairs and perform passing skills with one ball for every pair. One pair performs a different passing skill.

@ Students divide into groups of three to five and perform shooting skills. One group performs a different shooting skill.

Basketball Music Pass
Ages 8 and up

This active game combines basketball passing and shooting skills with aerobic fitness. The addition of music makes for very lively play.

Topics

@ Aerobic endurance

@ Locomotor skills

@ Manipulative skills

@ Cooperation

Objectives

@ Psychomotor—Demonstrate various kinds of basketball passes while moving.

@ Cognitive—Understand the application of force and absorption; explain how constant movement aids aerobic fitness.

@ Affective—Work cooperatively with several partners.

Equipment

@ 1 basketball or playground ball for each pair or group of three

@ Lively music

Safety

@ Make sure there is a clear path to pass the ball between partners or groups.

@ Do not pass over anyone's head.

Game

1. The class divides into pairs or groups of three.

2. Each pair or group receives one basketball or playground ball.

3. Play some lively music. When the music is on, the students pass the ball while moving continuously. When the music stops, the person with the ball passes to her predetermined partner (this rule is important because it keeps the children from holding the ball and waiting for the music to stop). In groups of three, keep the same passing order.

4. The person who receives the ball when the music stops dribbles to any basket, takes one shot at the basket, and dribbles back as quickly as possible before the music begins.

5. Students have 10 to 20 seconds to dribble, shoot, and come back.

6. After three or four rounds, students switch partners. One easy way to switch is for the person with the ball to stand still while everyone else moves to a new group or partner.

Variations

◎ Students use only one kind of basketball pass.

◎ The player takes a specific kind of shot.

◎ Students play for points. Each basket scores one point for the team. If the player returns to his group before the music begins, score one additional point.

◎ Students play for individual points. Each basket scores one point for the individual.

◎ Cooperative points—Total the baskets after two or three rounds. Try to beat the best score.

Bingo Ball
Ages 8 and up

Bingo is a very popular game. This game combines dribbling a basketball with playing bingo. The students practice their ball-handling skills while increasing their aerobic fitness. Substitute other ball-handling skills to change the game.

Topics

◎ Aerobic endurance

◎ Manipulative skills

◎ Cooperation

◎ Safety awareness

Objectives

◎ Psychomotor—Be able to dribble a ball with control while moving.

◎ Cognitive—Understand how much force to apply to control the ball; be able to explain the aerobic benefits of the game.

◎ Affective—Cooperate to keep the game moving and safe; appreciate individual differences in ability.

Equipment

◎ 1 poly spot for each student (use at least 3 colors of poly spots)

◎ 1 playground ball or basketball for each student

◎ 1 tennis ball for each student

Safety

◎ Dribble with control.

◎ Look in the direction you are going.

Game

1. Distribute one poly spot, one tennis ball, and one playground ball or basketball to each student, keeping one poly spot of each color.

2. The students begin in scatter formation. They place the tennis ball on the poly spot and sit behind the poly spot with the larger ball in their lap.

3. Designate one or more locations in the gymnasium or play area in which to place the tennis balls outside the play area. The students must be able to identify their balls, because the tennis balls act as game markers (they can use cardboard squares or index cards instead). It helps if the tennis balls have various letters or numbers written on them with magic marker. Otherwise, the students can place them in their own special spots.

4. The students place their tennis balls in the designated areas and remember where they placed them.

5. Designate other areas around the gymnasium as *b, i, n, g,* and *o* (see figure 5.1).

6. When the music starts or on the go signal, the students dribble their basketballs throughout the play area. When the music stops or on the stop signal, they find any empty poly spot and sit or stand on it. This step is repeated until the end of the game, when someone shouts, "Bingo!" See step 8 for details.

7. Close your eyes, mix up the poly spots, and choose one. All the students who are sitting or standing on that color retrieve their tennis ball (or other

game marker) from the tennis ball holding area and move it to the *b* area of the gymnasium.

8. Repeat steps 6 and 7, with students moving progressively to the next letter in order to spell out *bingo*. When a student moves his ball from the *b* through the other letters to the *o,* he shouts, "Bingo!" The round is over.

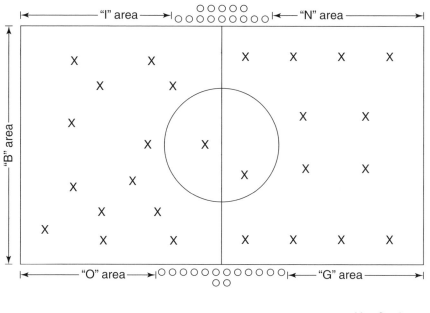

X = Students

O = Tennis Balls

Figure 5.1   Floor diagram of Bingo Ball.

Variations

- ◎ Have partners exchange playground balls for basketballs.
- ◎ Use various dribbling patterns.
- ◎ Students dribble and give high fives to other students.
- ◎ Students play Follow the Leader as they dribble the ball.
- ◎ Students try to tag their partners with their free hands.
- ◎ Use soccer and playground balls. The students dribble with their feet.

Bowling Pin Soccer
Ages 8 and up

This aerobic, fast-paced game helps teach the students how to control a soccer ball and how to defend against multiple attackers.

Topics

- Aerobic endurance
- Muscular strength and endurance
- Manipulative skills
- Cooperation

Objectives

- Psychomotor—Demonstrate dribbling and scoring skills with a soccer ball.
- Cognitive—Judge when to shoot a ball; understand defensive strategy.
- Affective—Cooperate to achieve group success; appreciate individual differences in ability.

Equipment

- 1 plastic bowling pin (or tennis ball can, milk jug, or small upside-down traffic cone) for every two students
- 1 soccer ball or playground ball for every two students (If available, use soccer ball trainers or another type of soft ball.)

Safety

- Kicks should be soft, short, and controlled.
- Look in the direction you are going.

Game

1. The class divides into pairs. Each pair receives a ball and a pin. An extra player may play alone and choose either a ball to play offense or a pin to play defense. This player should rotate equipment in order to have equal chances at offense and defense.

2. Each pair finds personal space in the play area.

3. On the go signal, the partner with the ball dribbles throughout the play area, attempting to knock over as many bowling pins as possible in a designated amount of time.

4. The partner without the ball defends the pin with her feet. If the pin is knocked down, the partner should immediately reset it.

5. Count one point for each pin knocked over. If the defender accidentally knocks over her pin, the dribbler closest to the pin gets the point.
6. The defender may not touch the pin with any body part while defending it, except to reset.
7. After a designated amount of time, the partners switch roles.

Variations

◎ Cooperative—Set up a minimum of 20 pins inside the play area. All players attempt to knock over the pins with the soccer balls. Time the round. Announce the amount of time it took to knock over all the pins. Time the students as they set up all the pins. Challenge the students to beat these times in the next round. Discuss strategies for speeding up success after each round.

◎ In the previous variation, choose three or four students to defend. They keep moving and try to keep the balls from knocking down the pins.

◎ Scooter—Distribute one gym scooter to each student. All previous rules remain the same except that students must remain on the scooters, and they may pick up the pins using only their feet. Discuss how this variation changes the focus from aerobic fitness to muscular strength and endurance.

Chinese Checkers
Ages 8 and up

The students become human checkers in this fast-paced game, which has four teams maneuvering from corner to corner.

Topics

◎ Aerobic endurance
◎ Manipulative skills
◎ Teamwork
◎ Cooperation
◎ Strategy

Objectives

◎ Psychomotor—Toss, throw, and catch various kinds of balls or manipulatives from various distances.
◎ Cognitive—Understand the application of force in order to throw and catch successfully; understand how to implement team strategy; be able to explain how to keep the game aerobic.
◎ Affective—Appreciate individual differences in ability.

Equipment

1 playground ball or other manipulative for every two or three students

Safety

⚠ ◎ Move with control.

◎ Watch for other students and equipment as you cross the middle of the play area.

Game

1. The class divides into four teams of five to nine players.

2. Give one ball (or other manipulative) to every two or three team members.

3. Set up teams in triangular formations in the four corners of the play area, as in a Chinese checkers board.

4. On the go signal, each team tries to get across the play area to the diagonally opposite corner and form their original triangle. Only the students with the balls may move. Since there are more players than balls, the players must figure out a way of moving across the play area and getting their teammates the ball. Do not tell the students how. Some of the ways may include throwing, tossing, bouncing, rolling, or handing the ball to one another.

5. Each team attempts to figure out the most efficient way of moving the whole team from corner to corner.

Variations

◎ Depending on age and skill level, vary the kinds of passes allowed.

◎ Vary the kind of equipment used, or use a variety of equipment in the same game.

◎ If a piece of equipment touches the floor, the last person who touched it goes back to the start.

◎ If someone does not make a successful catch, that person picks up the ball and goes back to the start.

◎ Only the students without a piece of equipment may move. The equipment may not touch the floor, and therefore the team passes equipment to one another until the whole team is set up in the opposite corner. A dropped piece of equipment requires both the passer and the catcher to go back to the start.

◎ Cooperative—Time how long it takes for all four teams to set up. See how many times each team can go back and forth in a given amount of time.

◎ Competitive—See which team crosses the play area successfully first. See which team goes back and forth the most times in a given amount of time.

Cooperative Partners
Ages 5 to 7

Partners work together to manipulate various pieces of equipment. The running keeps their heart rates up.

Topics

⊚ Aerobic endurance

⊚ Manipulative skills

⊚ Cooperation

Objectives

⊚ Psychomotor—Be able to manipulate a variety of objects with a partner.

⊚ Cognitive—Understand how much force to apply to an object in order to control its speed and distance.

⊚ Affective—Appreciate individual differences in manipulative skills; cooperate to achieve success.

Equipment

1 manipulative object for each pair or group of students (various kinds of balls, beanbags, hoops, and so forth)

Safety

⊚ Make sure the partners or groups have enough room to run around one another.

⊚ If more than one person is running around a partner, leave appropriate distance between runners.

Game

1. Students form pairs or groups of three.

2. Distribute one manipulative to each pair or group.

3. When the music is on, the partners pass the manipulative back and forth as quickly as possible, each trying to make sure the other partner can handle the exchange.

4. When the music stops, the person who does not have the object runs around the partner who does until the music begins again. If the object is on the floor when the music stops, the partner who is about to receive it remains still while his partner runs.

Variations

- Sit on the floor and roll a ball back and forth.
- Stand while bouncing and catching or tossing and catching a ball.
- Roll a hoop back and forth.
- Toss a beanbag.
- Toss a plastic bowling pin.
- Vary the distance between partners.
- Let the partners decide on an appropriate distance to achieve success.
- The partner with the manipulative does something while her partner is running around. For example, she can toss or bounce the ball, spin the hoop, balance the beanbag, and so forth.
- Each time the music stops, the person without the manipulative moves to a new partner. The person with the manipulative stays still and holds up one hand until a new partner arrives. As soon as the new partners get together, they may begin working together even if the music has not started yet.
- Establish a goal: "Can you make 100 successful catches by the time the game is over?"

Desert Island Volleyball
Ages 6 and up

Sometimes setting an imaginary scene creates an intriguing atmosphere for game playing. The imagery of the desert island adds incentive to successful practice and cooperation.

Topics

- Aerobic endurance
- Manipulative skills
- Volleyball skills
- Teamwork
- Cooperation

Objectives

- Psychomotor—Be able to throw or strike several types of balls or balloons accurately; move continuously for at least 10 minutes.

- Cognitive—Understand the application of force necessary to strike or throw a chosen manipulative with control; understand the aerobic nature of the game.
- Affective—Appreciate individual differences in ability; work to help a partner or group achieve success.

Equipment

- 1 balloon or ball for every two to three students (volleyballs, beach balls, volleyball trainers, slow-motion balls, playground balls, and so forth)
- Volleyball net or nets (optional)

Safety

- Instruct the students to keep space between their pair or group and other groups.
- Move with control.

Game

1. Place volleyball nets (if used) along the centerline or in the middle of the play area.
2. The students divide into pairs or groups of three.
3. Each pair or group begins at either end of the play area behind one of the lines. The lines may be the width lines of a basketball court. If lines are not available, use game markers such as traffic cones or poly spots.
4. Tell the students, "Behind the line on one side of the play area you are on a desert island with plenty of food, but no water. On the other side you are on a desert island with plenty of water, but no food."
5. The object of the game is for the students to cross the ocean to the other side. The ocean begins at the line on both ends of the play area. The nets are debris. The ball is the life preserver. The life preserver may never touch the ocean (floor). The life preserver travels over the net, whereas the students go under. If there is no net, students just travel back and forth between islands.
6. The person with the ball (life preserver) may not move. The person without the ball should judge the distance he can move away and still be able to receive the pass.
7. Students choose the manipulative according to age and ability.
8. Six- and seven-year-olds may toss or throw and then move.

9. Balloons must be passed, set, or spiked back and forth, with the partners or group in constant motion. Balls may be self-set and passed (forearm pass), set, spiked, or served to a partner who catches them.

10. If the ball or balloon drops, the students go back to the island they last left.

11. Once the students reach their destination, they may travel back and forth between the two islands. Each group or pair counts how many times they were able to go back and forth in the given time.

Variations

◎ After each completed trip, use pennies, marbles, puzzle pieces, or some other objects that students can collect and use as counters.

◎ Vary the way in which the students may strike the ball. Each ball may require a unique volleyball skill, or the students may choose their own skills.

◎ More advanced students may be asked to set the ball to each other continuously, but allow them to catch it as they approach the net so that one and then the other may pass underneath.

◎ After each successful or unsuccessful trip, allow the students to change equipment.

◎ After a given period of time, change partners or groups.

◎ Assign points to various skills. The harder the skill, the more points the partners or groups score.

◎ Cooperative—Add the total successful trips and try to beat the class score next time. See whether the class can complete more trips in the same amount of time.

◎ Competitive—Each pair or group tries for the best score.

◎ Change the equipment and play Desert Island Basketball, Football, Soccer, Lacrosse, Tennis, and so on.

Standards

◎ One—performs versatile striking or throwing skills.

◎ Two—understands the application of force when striking or throwing a ball; understands force absorption when catching or receiving a pass or strike.

◎ Three—understands the importance of volleyball as a resource for everyone regardless of age or ability; volleyball encourages family play; volleyball can often be found at a local YMCA or other youth groups.

◎ Four—understands that constant movement promotes aerobic fitness.

⑥ Five—focuses on cooperation and teamwork between partners or groups.

⑥ Six—works well with all partners or groups regardless of individual ability.

Differentiation

⑥ Respects the readiness level of each student (ball choice; type of strike—set, pass, or spike; distance traveled with each strike; speed of travel).

⑥ Offers advice to all students to improve growth (teacher walks around to each pair or group).

⑥ As students develop skills, they may escalate the degree of difficulty (teacher or students may change partners or groups, perform more difficult skills).

⑥ Assessment is ongoing and diagnostic.

Dispatcher
Ages 8 and up

Dispatcher is an exciting game that helps students learn how to work cooperatively with each other. The game may be played at a slow or quick pace. Quickening the pace makes it more aerobic.

Topics

⑥ Aerobic endurance

⑥ Balance

⑥ Agility

⑥ Cooperation

⑥ Teamwork

Objectives

⑥ Psychomotor—Be able to balance a playground ball between various body parts cooperatively with one or two other students.

⑥ Cognitive—Understand how to apply equal pressure to keep the ball from falling; understand the cooperative nature of the game; understand how to make the game more aerobic.

⑥ Affective—Work cooperatively as a team to achieve a group goal.

Equipment

⊚ Approximately 1 playground ball for each student

⊚ 8 to 12 hoops

Safety

⊚ Communicate with each other when working together.

⊚ Avoid collisions.

Game

1. The class discusses the job of a dispatcher. Explain that the students will be working in pairs or groups of three, attempting to distribute the balls evenly into each hoop. The hoops are homes, the balls are delivery packages, two students together are a van, and three together are a truck.

2. Choose four to six students to act as dispatchers.

3. Two or three dispatchers place a ball between body parts of two (pair) or three (group) students so that they can hold it without using their hands. The other dispatchers work in the hoop area.

4. Once they have their balls, the vans and trucks attempt to cross the play area and deliver the packages into the hoops (homes) without using their hands. However, if the package falls, the students may pick up the ball and take it back to the starting line. They may begin again as soon as a dispatcher positions the ball.

5. If the ball does not stay in the hoop when placed down, the van or truck calls one of the dispatchers who is standing near the hoops to place the ball between their bodies so they can try again. These dispatchers also act as judges to make sure the vans and trucks do not use their hands to place the ball in the hoop.

6. Time the event to see how long it takes the class to distribute all the balls evenly into all the hoops. If one hoop has four and the rest have three, it is fine. However, if one hoop has four and another has one or two, a ball must be moved. The dispatchers can help direct the vans or trucks.

7. For the next round, choose new dispatchers and see whether the class can beat its best time.

Variations

⊚ The dispatcher can select the body parts to place the ball between.

⊚ The vans or trucks can tell the dispatcher where to place the ball.

⊚ Everyone must place the ball in the same spot. For example, students are only allowed to move back to back.

⊚ Each van or truck has a driver. The driver does not touch the ball. The students who are the van or truck close their eyes. The driver steers the van or truck by placing her hands on their outside shoulders.

⊚ Aerobic—Place the ball between two students' shoulders. See how quickly they place all the balls in the hoops. Time the event and play again, trying to beat the best time. If you use this variation, allow the children to use their hands to place the ball. In this case have fewer dispatchers, since you won't need any in the hoop area. Discuss why this variation makes the game more aerobic.

Down the Chimney
Ages 5 and up

Down the Chimney was created for the holiday season, but students may play it at any time by simply changing the name. They can play individually, in pairs, or in small groups. You may prearrange distances from the target or leave them to the students' discretion.

Topics

⊚ Aerobic endurance

⊚ Overhand throw

⊚ Teamwork

⊚ Cooperation

Objectives

⊚ Psychomotor—Be able to throw a ball accurately from various distances, catch a ball from various distances, and move quickly without a ball.

⊚ Cognitive—Understand the force necessary to throw a ball accurately; understand correct form for the overhand throw; explain what aspect of the game promotes aerobic fitness.

⊚ Affective—Accept individual differences in ability; work with one or more partners to achieve success.

Equipment

⊚ 50 to 100 tennis balls

⊚ 1 container to keep the balls in

⊚ 16 or more hoops

Safety

⚠️ ⓖ Make sure there is a clear path to the target before throwing a ball.
ⓖ Move with control.
ⓖ Know where the other children are before throwing a ball.

Game

1. Place the tennis balls in a container in the center of the play area.

2. Attach eight or more hoops to a gym wall or yard fence spread throughout the play area. Tie them to the fence with string or attach to the wall with tape. Tape or tie some hoops higher on the wall or fence than others so that they are at various heights from the floor or ground.

3. Place other hoops on the floor, either to the left or right of the hung hoops.

4. Allow each student to take one tennis ball and scatter throughout the play area.

5. Tell the students that the balls are presents, the hoops on the wall are chimneys, and the hoops on the floor are the children's homes.

6. On the go signal, the students attempt to throw their balls (presents) into a hoop (chimney) on the wall. If successful, they place the present in the hoop on the floor (a child's home) and go back for another present. If unsuccessful, they retrieve the present and move on to another chimney. This is a good opportunity to teach the term *challenge by choice*. The children pick the distance from their target according to each individual's challenge level.

7. Tell the students that they should try to even out the presents so that all the children get almost the same amount.

8. For safety purposes, explain that no one should aim at a chimney while another student is directly in front of them or is placing a present in a home.

9. When all the presents are distributed, stop the game and see whether they distributed a fairly even amount into each chimney. Have them collect the balls, one at a time, and return them to the center container. Play the game again. See whether they can beat their best time or better distribute the presents.

Variations

ⓖ Work in pairs. One student passes the ball to another. The person with the ball may not move. If students drop the ball, they return it to the container. Each pair must make at least one or two passes before taking a shot at a chimney. Allow less skilled students to roll the ball to each other. Alternate shots.

- Use the first variation. Instead of hoop targets, use basketball hoops. Divide the students into pairs or groups of three. The students pick a ball from the center and pass the ball until they get close enough to the basket to shoot. They take one shot. If the ball goes in, they place it in the hoop on the floor near that basket. If they miss, they may take turns shooting until the ball goes in. Or you can have students bring the ball back to the start and choose another ball.

- Use different kinds of balls or different kinds of targets. For example, in the previous variation, use basketballs.

- Tape lines or place poly spots at various distances from each chimney. Students may not cross the lines to throw the ball. This variation allows for various grade levels and abilities.

- When students are collecting the presents, tell them they have become grinches. They want to collect the presents from the hoop homes as quickly as possible. They must take only one at a time. Time them to see how quickly they return all the balls to the original container.

- Time the event. Challenge students to do better next time.

Elves Versus Grinches

Ages 8 and up

Here is an excellent holiday game that students can play at any time by changing the name of the game. This game provides strategic training in zone defenses and helps students learn to move without the ball.

Topics

- Aerobic endurance
- Manipulative skills
- Teamwork
- Strategy

Objectives

- Psychomotor—Be able to throw and catch a ball from various distances; move quickly without the ball.

- Cognitive—Understand the amount of force necessary to throw a ball accurately; understand how to move into open spaces to receive a ball; begin to understand the concept of a zone defense; be able to explain how to make the game more aerobic.

- Affective—Appreciate individual differences in ability; work together to achieve a team goal.

Equipment

⊚ 1 foam or Gator Skin ball for every six players

⊚ 2 hoops for each team

Safety

⊚ Stay in your own area.

⊚ If a ball leaves your area, retrieve it carefully so as not to interfere with other games.

⊚ Look in the direction you are going.

Game

1. The class divides into groups of six. The leftover students become the referees.

2. Hang each team's two hoops on opposite ends of the play area, slightly higher than the height of hands held high above the head. Use the width of the gymnasium or play area.

3. The balls are the presents. The hoops are the chimneys. The grinches protect the children's chimneys, and the elves protect their own chimneys.

4. There are four elves and two grinches in each group. The elves are trying to deliver the presents to the children by throwing the ball into the children's hung hoop. There are two grinches. The grinches are trying to stop them by intercepting the ball, blocking the throw, or throwing the ball back into the elves' chimney on the opposite end.

5. The game begins with the elves in possession of the ball near their own chimney. The grinches may begin anywhere they like.

6. The students may not move with the ball. The pivot foot must remain still.

7. If one team drops the ball, the other team takes possession.

8. After each shot, the other team takes possession.

9. If the elves score, the game continues until the elves score again. At this point the two grinches become elves, any referee waiting becomes a grinch, and two of the elves become referees. If no one is waiting, the two grinches rotate with two of the elves.

10. If the grinches score, they immediately rotate and become elves.

Variations

⊚ Vary the number of players.

⊚ Play three versus three, four versus four, and so forth.

⊚ Vary the height of the target.

⊚ Use fewer courts if space is limited. Allow two groups to compete on the same court with different-colored balls. In this case the two groups should go in opposite directions, because one team's elf chimney is the other team's grinch chimney and vice versa.

⊚ Change the name of the game and play it anytime.

Fearsome Five

Ages 8 and up

This keep-away game encourages the students to work together while keeping their heart rates up.

Topics

⊚ Aerobic endurance

⊚ Manipulative skills

⊚ Safety awareness

Objectives

⊚ Psychomotor—Manipulate a ball with the feet while moving and changing directions.

⊚ Cognitive—Understand the need to control the ball's speed in order to change direction; understand the need for safety in a fast-moving game; understand the strategy of working together; understand the aerobic benefits of the game.

⊚ Affective—Appreciate individual differences in ball-handling ability.

Equipment

⊚ 1 tennis ball for each student

⊚ 1 box, bag, or crate in which to store the tennis balls

⊚ 1 stopwatch

Safety

⦿ Pick up balls when they are away from the feet of others.

⦿ Look in the direction you are going.

⦿ Move with control.

Game

1. Distribute one tennis ball to each student.
2. The students dribble the ball throughout the play area as in soccer, using only the feet.
3. Choose five students to return their tennis balls. These five students become the Fearsome Five. Their job is to pick up all the balls as the other students attempt to keep the balls away from them. Remind students that for safety reasons, they must never try to pick up a ball until it is away from someone else's foot.
4. As the Fearsome Five collect the tennis balls, they may take them to a central location and place them in a crate, box, or bag.
5. Time the Fearsome Five. When they have collected all the balls, announce the time.
6. Choose a new group to be the Fearsome Five. Challenge that group to beat the time of the first Fearsome Five. Each new Fearsome Five attempts to beat the best time.
7. Rotate through the class until each student has a turn to become part of the Fearsome Five.
8. Physical contact is strictly prohibited. Establish a penalty box for students who break this rule.
9. Inform the students that when they lose their ball, they are not out of the game. They should try to help the rest of the class keep the balls away from the Fearsome Five by serving as receivers to pass the balls to.

Variations

⦿ Use other types of balls.

⦿ Instead of kicking the balls, the students can toss or throw the balls to each other. Begin this variation with one ball for every two students. If one of the Fearsome Five tags someone while that student has a ball in his hand, the latter must hand it over to the tagger. This rule discourages students from holding on to balls.

Ice Cream Cones
Ages 5 and up

This game provides a unique variation on tossing and catching. The constant motion provides a good aerobic workout.

Topics

- Aerobic endurance
- Locomotor skills
- Manipulative skills
- Cooperation

Objectives

- Psychomotor—Perform locomotor skills while holding ice cream cones (traffic cones) (ages 5 and 6). Toss and catch various manipulatives using a small traffic cone to receive the toss; perform several locomotor skills while tossing and catching a manipulative (ages 7 and up).

- Cognitive—Understand the proper force necessary to control a toss; understand how to steady and soften a receptacle to catch a manipulative (absorption); be able to explain the aerobic nature of the game.

- Affective—Cooperate to keep the activity moving and safe; accept individual differences in ability.

Equipment

- 1 small traffic cone for each student
- Fleece balls, beanbags, playground balls, or other manipulatives that students can catch using a small traffic cone

Safety

- Move and toss the manipulative with control.
- Look in the direction you are going.

Game

1. Tell the students that their traffic cone is an ice cream cone. They will be using their cones to hold the ice cream (playground ball or other manipulative).

2. Each student receives one playground ball. If you have balls of various colors, pretend that each color is a flavor of ice cream.

3. Students walk, gallop, skip, and so forth throughout the play area without dropping their ice cream.

4. Older students attempt to toss and catch their ice cream on the cone. They try catching it after one bounce, two bounces, three bounces, and so on. Some students may be able to toss and catch without any bounces. Instead of using one hand to toss, they can try tossing by lifting the cone so that the ball flies off.

5. Students may try various locomotor skills while tossing and catching their manipulatives.

6. The students count their own consecutive tosses and catches or their own total catches.

Variations

◉ Use other manipulatives. Tell the students the ice cream is melting. When using smaller manipulatives, the students must toss and catch without letting their ice cream hit the floor.

◉ Students work in small groups. Each group totals their consecutive or total catches.

◉ If a student drops a manipulative, she freezes. This student may be unfrozen if another student (while still tossing and catching) walks over, stops tossing and catching, picks up the dropped item, and hands it back to the frozen student.

◉ Students work in groups of three or four, using only one manipulative per group. Challenge each group to move from one given location to another without dropping the manipulative. Playground balls may bounce once or twice. The person holding the manipulative may not move. Students can also toss playground balls off the ice cream cone without using any hands.

◉ Use different-colored playground balls. The students walk throughout the play area holding their ice cream cones with one hand. When the music stops or you give the stop signal, the students toss their ice cream in the air by a sudden lift of the cone and attempt to catch another flavor on one or more bounces.

Multiple Partners
Ages 5 and up

Many options exist for finding partners. It is wonderful to see children work cooperatively with various peers. Multiple Partners allows the students to work with a variety of people for brief periods. The game helps students grow more comfortable working with others.

Topics

- ◎ Aerobic endurance
- ◎ Muscular strength and endurance
- ◎ Flexibility
- ◎ Manipulative skills
- ◎ Cooperation
- ◎ Collaborative skills
- ◎ Leadership skills
- ◎ Communication skills

Objectives

- ◎ Psychomotor—Be able to perform various locomotor skills and partner stunts.
- ◎ Cognitive—Understand that there are many ways to find partners; understand the components of fitness.
- ◎ Affective—Seek to cooperate with a large and diversified group of people.

Equipment

None, 1 piece of equipment for everyone, or 1 piece for every two people

Safety

- ◎ Move with control.
- ◎ Find safe areas in which to perform skills and exercises.

Game

1. Students find various partners according to each instruction. Here are some examples:
   - ◎ Can you find a partner who was born in the same month as you and sit down next to that partner? This is partner 1.
   - ◎ Can you find another partner who has the same color of socks as you and sit down next to that partner? This is partner 2.
   - ◎ Can you find a partner who was born on the same numbered day of any month as you or someone born within two days of you? This is partner 3.
   - ◎ Can you find a partner who has the same favorite food as you? This is partner 4.
   - ◎ Can you find a partner who likes the same TV show or has the same favorite book as you? This is partner 5.

2. Those students unable to find partners in a designated amount of time go to the skill building area for communication (an assigned area where the students can talk to each other or quickly agree to become partners). If there is one student without a partner, that person can either have an imaginary partner for one round or make one group of three.

Variations

Play any of these variations or combine them.

◎ Ask students to quickly find the appropriate partner when you call out a number. When you call out the number 5, they find partner 5. When you call out the number 1, they find partner 1. The students move from partner to partner; call these numbers quickly.

◎ Have students find other sets of partners with similar interests as a way to form groups.

◎ Ask the children to perform various activities with each partner. For example, with partner 1 they can play Follow the Leader. With partner 2, they can scratch each other's backs. With partner 3, they can each perform curl-ups. With partner 4, they can give each other a shoulder massage. With partner 5, they can take a tennis ball and play catch. Other possible partner activities include standing on the partner's feet while the partner takes them for a walk and toe-fencing, in which partners try to tap each other's toes.

　◎ Have students choose other fitness activities with each partner. Here are some examples: Take turns doing a push-up, invent a fitness routine, perform three stretches, get a jump rope and perform a jump rope routine with the partner, or invent a fitness routine using a tennis or playground ball.

◎ Ask the children to take a piece of equipment and do something with the equipment.

　◎ Partner 1 is their tossing and catching the beanbag partner. They may toss one beanbag at a time or toss both at the same time.

　◎ Partner 2 is their throwing the beanbag partner. Partners use only one beanbag and throw to each other.

　◎ Partner 3 is their sliding the beanbag partner. Partners slide one or both beanbags to each other.

　◎ Partner 4 is their hitting the penny partner. Students place one beanbag down on the floor between partners. Partners take turns tossing the other beanbag above shoulder height, trying to hit the target beanbag. Each hit receives one point.

　◎ Partner 5 is their tossing the beanbag over the head partner. Partners use one beanbag and alternate turning their back to the partner and tossing the beanbag over the head. Partners receive one point each time the beanbag is caught.

⊚ As in the first variation, after the students have five partners, keep them moving by calling out a different number every couple of minutes or less. Do not wait for everyone to find his partner before changing the partner number. Changing the number often encourages the students to move quickly. The students try to remember who each partner was and what activity they did with that partner. When they get to their partner, they always do the same activity with that partner.

⊚ Only begin with partner 1. After students have found partner 1, explain what they will always do with this partner. Next, ask the students to find partner 2, and explain a different activity with this partner. Keep this pattern up until the students have five or more partners, with different activities for each partner. In order to help them remember who their partners were and what activity they performed with that partner, have them return to earlier partners before they are actually given all their partners.

Pirate Ball
Ages 8 and up

Students attempt to steal the ball from others during this fast-paced aerobic game. Children particularly love the variation in which the teacher becomes the pirate.

Topics

⊚ Aerobic endurance

⊚ Manipulative skills

⊚ Cooperation

⊚ Safety awareness

Objectives

⊚ Psychomotor—Dribble a ball without looking directly at it, while moving throughout general space.

⊚ Cognitive—Understand the importance of dribbling while not looking directly at the ball; be able to explain the aerobic benefits of the game.

⊚ Affective—Appreciate individual differences in ball-handling skills; appreciate the need for safety in a game situation.

Equipment

1 basketball, soccer ball, or playground ball for each student

Safety

⚠

- ◎ Physically touching anyone else is strictly forbidden.
- ◎ Look in the direction you are going.
- ◎ Move with control.

Game

1. Each student receives one ball.
2. The students practice dribbling the ball throughout the play area.
3. Remove the ball from one to five players. These players become the pirates. The pirates move throughout the play area attempting to steal the balls from the other players, using their hands for basketballs and their feet for soccer balls. Playground balls may be used as basketballs or soccer balls.
4. After stealing a ball, pirates return it to the owner.
5. After 1 to 3 minutes, new pirates are chosen.
6. The students must keep their heads up while dribbling.

Variations

- ◎ Pirates steal the balls as before. The person whose ball was stolen becomes the new pirate.
- ◎ Everyone has a ball. Everyone dribbles and, using the free hand (basketball) or free foot (soccer), attempts to force others to lose control of their balls. A student counts one point each time she causes another student to lose control of his ball, as long as she maintains control of her own ball.
- ◎ You are the only pirate.
- ◎ Vary the locomotor skills.
- ◎ Students work in pairs or small groups of three or four with one ball. In addition to dribbling, they may also pass the ball to each other to avoid a pirate.
- ◎ Use only one kind of ball or use various kinds in the same game.

Quick Partners
Ages 5 and up

Here is another excellent game to encourage students to work with numerous partners while keeping their heart rates up.

Topics

- ◎ Aerobic endurance
- ◎ Locomotor skills
- ◎ Cooperation
- ◎ Collaborative skills
- ◎ Leadership skills
- ◎ Communication skills

Objectives

- ◎ Psychomotor—Be able to perform various locomotor skills alone and with a partner.
- ◎ Cognitive—Understand the importance of finding a partner quickly.
- ◎ Affective—Seek to cooperate with a large or diverse group of people.

Equipment

None, except in the last variation

Safety

- ◎ Look in the direction you are going.
- ◎ Move with control.

Game

1. The students move throughout general space according to your directions.
2. On a given signal, the students stop and find a partner as quickly as possible.
3. After finding a partner, the two students move in tandem, either one behind the other or one beside the other.
4. Students unable to find a partner go to a centralized area. If one student is left over, that student may join any pair.

Variations

- Give the students 15 to 20 seconds to find a partner. Keep decreasing the amount of time the students have until they have only 2 to 3 seconds. Those students who fail to find a partner in the allotted time must sit out one round of movement. An alternative is for you to assign them a partner.
- Ask the students to find a partner who is closest to them when the partner signal is given.
- On the partner signal, ask to the students to spin around once and make eye contact with the first person they see. That person becomes their partner.
- Assign each student number 1 or number 2. At the partner signal, the 1s choose a 2 or the 2s choose a 1. In this variation only the 1s or 2s are moving, whereas the others are standing still with one hand raised or are performing an exercise.
- Choose about 25 percent of the class to be facilitators. At the partner signal, the facilitators quickly choose partners for everyone by bringing two people together.
- At the partner signal, the students play tag. As soon as a student tags someone or someone tags him, that person becomes his partner.
- Add equipment to the game.

Soccer Bump
Ages 8 and up

Soccer Bump works very well for practicing soccer dribbling skills. The variations allow for great fun and a lot of movement.

Topics

- Aerobic endurance
- Manipulative skills
- Cooperation

Objectives

- Psychomotor—Dribble a soccer ball with control while jogging throughout general space.
- Cognitive—Understand how much force to apply to a moving ball in order to control it; be able to explain the aerobic benefits of the game.
- Affective—Appreciate individual differences in dribbling skills.

Equipment

1 soccer or playground ball for each student

Safety

⊚ Look in the direction you are going.

⊚ Move with control.

⊚ Keep the soccer ball close to your feet.

Game

1. Students begin in scatter formation.

2. Each student receives one ball.

3. On the go signal, students dribble their ball throughout the play area, attempting to control it and not allowing their ball to touch another ball, anyone, or anything.

4. Ask the students to keep track of how many times their ball touches anyone or anything.

5. Play for approximately 2 minutes. Challenge the students to improve their performances in the next round.

Variations

⊚ Instead of trying to avoid the other balls, students see how many times they can make their ball touch another ball (bump) while still keeping control.

⊚ While dribbling and avoiding or touching other balls, students see how fast they can stop or trap their ball when you give a set signal.

⊚ While dribbling throughout the play area, students exchange balls with other students by simultaneously passing to each other. They see how many exchanges they can make before you give the stop signal.

⊚ While keeping control of their ball, students try to force other students to lose control of their ball without touching either them or their ball.

⊚ Choose two to four students to be trappers. The trappers try to place one foot on top of any ball. As soon as they make a trap, they give the ball back and move on. The dribblers attempt any of the above games while avoiding the trappers. Trappers score one point for each trap. After a designated amount of time, exchange trappers.

Titanic
Ages 8 and up

This cooperative game, based on the famous ship *Titanic,* encourages students to work together in order to achieve a group goal. Encourage students to keep moving in order to keep this game as aerobic as possible.

Topics

- Aerobic endurance
- Manipulative skills
- Cooperation
- Teamwork

Objectives

- Psychomotor—Be able to toss and catch a ball from various distances; roll a ball accurately from various distances.
- Cognitive—Understand the application of force necessary to make an accurate toss, throw, or roll; be able to explain how to make the game more aerobic.
- Affective—Work together to achieve a group goal; appreciate individual differences in ability.

Equipment

- 1 playground ball for every five or six students
- Traffic cones to mark the areas
- 1 stopwatch

Safety

- Look in the direction you are going.
- Throw balls carefully so as not to hit anyone.

Game

1. Use traffic cones to mark off an area. Floor tape (that doesn't leave a mark) can be used to tape the word *Titanic* on the floor inside the cones. Designate another area across the play area to be land; the rest of the floor is water.

2. All the students begin on the area marked *Titanic*. The ship has hit an iceberg and is sinking. Lifeboats are frozen and inoperable. The only way to safety is to use the life preservers (playground balls) on board.

3. The object of the game is to move all the students safely to dry land in as little time as possible.

4. Students may enter the water only if they have a life preserver. No more than two students may share one preserver.

5. A student may cross to land only if touching a life preserver.

6. Students may stay still (tread water) without a preserver. They must move their arms and legs vigorously when standing still.

7. Time the event. Challenge the students to beat their best time.

Variations

⑥ The students may return life preservers in any way they can think of. For example, they may cross to dry land and roll the preserver back to the ship. If the preserver does not reach the ship or goes to the side or past the ship, that preserver is out of the game unless retrieved by any student carrying another preserver. Students may also carry the preservers back to the *Titanic* and pick up another student.

⑥ The life preservers may not touch the water, and students may not share a preserver. In this case the students must throw or toss the preservers to each other without letting them hit the water. If a preserver hits the water, the student who is closest to it must swim to it (jog while rotating arms), retrieve it, and start from the *Titanic* again. Alternatively, the student who threw the preserver may jump in the water, swim to it, and return to the *Titanic*.

⑥ Use various pieces of equipment. For example, if students are working on volleyball passing, they can use volleyball trainers.

⑥ If students are practicing a particular kind of pass, allow only that kind of pass, such as chest passes only.

⑥ Instead of using balls, students use gym scooters as lifeboats. Scooters can also be placed under mats to make larger lifeboats.

⑥ Competitive—Divide the class into four teams. Give each team an equal number of life preservers. See which team successfully gets its whole group to dry land the fastest.

Turn Off the TV
Ages **7** and up

Too much TV and too many video games contribute to the epidemic of childhood obesity. Here is a game that encourages the students to exercise and to help each other by turning off the TV.

Topics

- Aerobic endurance
- Muscular strength and endurance
- Locomotor skills
- Manipulative skills
- Cooperation
- Strategy

Objectives

- Psychomotor—Demonstrate ability to control several pieces of equipment; chase and flee with or without gym scooters.
- Cognitive—Understand how to apply offensive and defensive strategy to a game situation; choose exercises and games that promote fitness.
- Affective—Cooperate to keep the game moving and safe; work to accomplish a team goal.

Equipment

- Several kinds of balls
- 6 to 10 hoops
- 5 to 10 jump ropes
- 3 to 5 foam balls
- 7 to 11 scooter boards
- 4 to 6 beanbags
- Magazine pictures attached to a hoop (the TV)
- Traffic cones or poly spots to mark off the TV area

Game

1. Show the students the hoop with the magazine pictures and explain that this is the TV. People stare blankly at it instead of having fun playing and communicating.

2. Place the TV at one end of the play area (if possible, set on a hoop holder). Place the traffic cones or poly spots in front of the TV. The TV addicts may not cross this line.

3. The space between the TV area and the center of the play area is a vast TV wasteland.

4. Choose three to five students to be the guardians of the tube. These are the TV addicts. Give each one a foam ball and a gym scooter. They live in the wasteland area between the TV area and the centerline.

5. Choose one student to be the TV watcher. This student sits in front of the TV, facing away from the other students (see figure 5.2).

6. The rest of the students are playing happily in the far half of the play area. They can jump rope, toss a ball to each other or against the wall, play with the hoops, or do various fitness exercises. However, they feel guilty because one of their friends is stranded alone, wasting his time watching TV. They wish to rescue their friend.

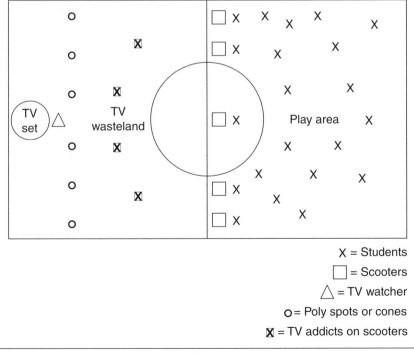

X = Students

☐ = Scooters

△ = TV watcher

o = Poly spots or cones

𝕏 = TV addicts on scooters

Figure 5.2   Floor diagram for Turn Off the TV.

7. Place scooters, one more than there are guardians, on the centerline. In effect, this is a game of four against three or five against four, and so on. Choose students to start the game as rescuers on the scooters. The others may get in line behind them or play with the equipment.

8. Once the rescuers cross the play area's centerline, the guardians may tag them with the foam balls. When tagged, rescuers stand and carefully carry their scooter to the centerline. If another rescuer is waiting, they pass the scooter to that person. If no one is in line, they may start again.

9. If anyone in the group succeeds in getting by the guards untagged, that student turns the TV around, thus freeing the captured TV watcher and ending the round.

10. Choose new guardians, new rescuers, and a new TV watcher.

Variations

⑥ Instead of one student freeing the TV watcher, two students free him. If one rescuer gets through, she holds one end of the TV hoop. When the second rescuer gets through, they turn the TV around together.

⑥ Set a time limit. If the TV watcher is not freed in 3 to 5 minutes, choose new guardians and a new TV watcher.

⑥ Instead of using scooters, students use various locomotor skills to get across the wasteland.

⑥ Do not assign anyone to be the TV watcher. Make this an imaginary person.

Vampire Ball
Ages 8 and up

Vampire Ball sounds like a Halloween game, but it is actually based on a game called Killer. Students can play it anytime. It is wonderful for teaching children to dribble with their heads up while moving throughout general space.

Topics

⑥ Aerobic endurance
⑥ Manipulative skills
⑥ Cooperation

Objectives

⊚ Psychomotor—Be able to dribble a ball continuously with either hand.

⊚ Cognitive—Understand the reason for dribbling with either hand without looking directly at the ball; understand the aerobic nature of the game.

⊚ Affective—Appreciate individual differences in ability; appreciate the importance of honesty when playing a game.

Equipment

Use 1 playground ball or basketball for each student. Using basketballs is preferable because the skill is dribbling. However, if there are not enough basketballs for the class, give half the class playground balls. Each person with a playground ball has a partner with a basketball. Every 2 to 3 minutes, they exchange with their partner.

Safety

⊚ Look in the direction you are going.

⊚ Move with control.

Game

1. Distribute one basketball or playground ball to each student.

2. Tell the students that one of them will become a vampire. The vampire will attempt to turn the humans into vampires.

3. Designate a place in the play area where the students can sit either in a circle or along a line (the sideline of a basketball court works well). They all sit facing the same direction, with the balls held still in their laps.

4. Students close their eyes. Pick a vampire by walking behind the students and tapping someone on the shoulder. Nobody knows who the vampire is.

5. On the go signal, the students dribble while shaking hands with other students (try to have them switch to the left hand and shake with right hands).

6. If two humans shake hands, nothing happens. When a vampire shakes a hand, he tickles the other student's palm with one finger, making the other a vampire. If two vampires shake hands, they both turn human. Only the chief vampire (the one picked originally) never turns human.

7. At the end of each 2- to 3-minute round, pick three students to guess who the original vampire was. If using playground balls and basketballs, students exchange once during each round.

8. Tell the students they must shake hands with anyone who offers them a hand. Honesty is very important.

Variations

- Play for points. Award 5 points to the original vampire, 5 points to anyone who is a human at the end of the round, and 10 points to anyone who guesses the identity of the original vampire.

- Allow a vampire to take one shot at a basket from close range. If she makes the basket, she turns back into a human. If she misses, she must remain a vampire for the entire round.

- Use other methods of turning others into a vampire: Two students look eye to eye, but a vampire winks, makes a monster face, shows teeth, and so forth.

- Vary the equipment. For example, students play the same game with soccer balls.

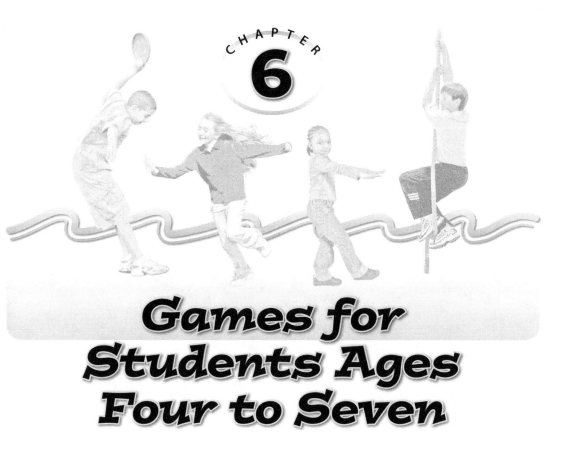

6

Games for Students Ages Four to Seven

The games in this chapter are designed primarily for younger students. They focus heavily on spatial awareness and locomotor skills, two building blocks necessary for achieving success in games and sports. The children should practice moving at various speeds, directions, pathways, and levels. If you add equipment, older students can play many of these games.

Abracadabra

Young children love to pretend. You will be the magician. The children use their imaginations to move throughout general space.

Topics

- ⊚ Aerobic endurance
- ⊚ Locomotor skills
- ⊚ Interpretive movement
- ⊚ Spatial awareness

Objectives

- ⊚ Psychomotor—Be able to use several locomotor skills to interpret movement.
- ⊚ Cognitive—Understand that there are various ways to interpret movement.
- ⊚ Affective—Seek to cooperate to enjoy a group game; appreciate qualities of individual movement.

Equipment

None, or a prop to use as a magic wand

Safety

- ⊚ Move with control.
- ⊚ Look in the direction you are going.

Game

1. Say, "I am a magician. This is my magic wand. When I wave my magic wand and say the magic word, 'Abracadabra!' you will become whatever I turn you into."

2. Wave the wand and turn the students into frogs, rabbits, horses, tigers, dogs, cats, snakes, robots, screwdrivers, cars, trucks, trains, planes, snowflakes, rain, hurricanes, balls, tops, pogo sticks, jumping beans, teachers, and so forth. The quicker and more often you change the named thing, the more fun the children have.

3. The students interpret the way they believe that named thing would move. They move throughout general space as this noun until you pause the action and say, "Abracadabra!" again.

4. This game presents an excellent opportunity to teach the difference between nouns and verbs. If you ask the children to gallop, there is no interpretation; therefore, it is a verb.

Variations

- Hold up signs with nouns written on them. The students read each sign and interpret the movement.
- Ask the children to interpret the noun at various speeds, levels, pathways, or directions. Here's an example: A snake at a low level means the children mostly slither on the floor (I always say afterward, "Thanks for cleaning my floor!"), but a snake at a high level means the children stand and use their arms to make a snake motion.
- The students can move with one or more partners to interpret the movement. For example, they may want to join up to become a long train.
- Students find partners and play Follow the Leader with their partners as they interpret the noun's movement.
- Students find partners and play Partner Tag using the locomotor skill the students have just interpreted. One student is It; students take turns being It. When one is tagged, they reverse roles. Each time a student makes a tag, he counts to three to give his partner a chance to get away.

Alphabet Soup

This game integrates language arts and movement.

Topics

- Aerobic endurance
- Locomotor skills
- Cooperation
- Letter recognition
- Spatial awareness

Objectives

- Psychomotor—Demonstrate several kinds of locomotor skills while moving safely throughout general space.
- Cognitive—Recognize uppercase and lowercase letters; spell simple to complex words; know how to move safely.
- Affective—Work cooperatively to achieve a group goal.

Equipment

- Oak tag or cardboard with the letters of the alphabet written individually on each piece
- 26 hoops

⚅ 50 or more tennis balls with uppercase and lowercase letters written on each one (Having more of the popular letters works well and allows these tennis balls to be used for many other games, like Scrabble Fitness.)

Safety

⚅ Move carefully when searching for the balls so as not to step on them.

⚅ Look in the direction you are going.

⚅ Move with control.

Game

Part 1

1. Each student receives one hoop and one letter. If there are less than 26 students, some students may receive an extra letter. If there are more than 26 students, some students may share a letter.

2. Students say the letters as they get them and find personal space, where they sit inside their hoops and place the letters on the floor in front of them inside the hoop. Any student with an extra letter uses two hoops.

3. Explain that the students will make some alphabet soup. Each time the music starts, or on the go signal, the students demonstrate a different locomotor skill throughout general space. They move without touching the soup's ingredients (the hoops or letters).

4. When the music stops, or on the stop signal, they stand still. Call out an ingredient: "Find a letter that begins your first name." The students find the hoop with that letter and sit inside the hoop. If others have the same letter, they share the hoop by placing one or two body parts inside the hoop.

5. The students then return to their original hoops.

6. Play begins again with a different ingredient.

Part 2

1. Explain that the soup needs additional ingredients. Roll out all of the tennis balls. Ask the students not to touch the balls unless they end up inside a hoop. The students can then roll these balls outside of the hoops (see figure 6.1).

2. Tell the students to gather the ingredients for the soup by finding the balls with the letter that matches the one in their hoop. When they find a ball, they place it in their hoop and look for another one. After a while, ask them to pick up any one ball and find the proper hoop.

3. When all the balls are in the proper hoops and the students are sitting in their original hoops, the soup is done.

4. Time the event and play again. The students see whether they can beat their best time.

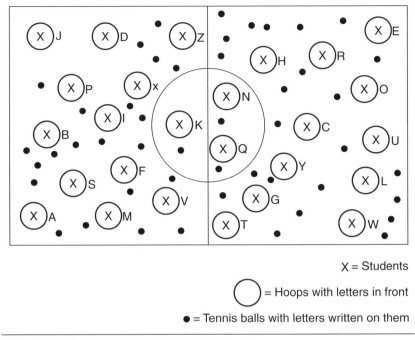

X = Students

◯ = Hoops with letters in front

● = Tennis balls with letters written on them

Figure 6.1 Floor diagram for part 2 of Alphabet Soup.

Camouflage

This is an outstanding game when played in a gymnasium with a brown floor. It is movement for the sheer joy of moving.

Topics

- ◎ Aerobic endurance
- ◎ Locomotor skills
- ◎ Cooperation
- ◎ Spatial awareness

Objectives

- ◎ Psychomotor—Demonstrate several locomotor skills while moving safely.
- ◎ Cognitive—Understand how similar colors can hide an object; understand how to move at various speeds to control breathing.
- ◎ Affective—Appreciate the need to move safely.

Equipment

10 to 50 pennies or some other small objects that blend into the color of the gymnasium floor

Safety

⊚ Look in the direction you are going.

⊚ Move with control.

Game

1. Ask the students to hide their eyes.

2. Hide a penny somewhere on the floor of the gymnasium.

3. Tell the students to try to find the penny.

4. Next, increase the number of pennies for the students to find. While the students are hiding their eyes, either hide the pennies or simply toss them out and let them roll until they stop. On the go signal, the students try to find all of the pennies.

5. After a penny is found, the student hands the penny to you before continuing to look for more pennies. Count the pennies so that you know when all are found.

6. After all the pennies are found, a new round begins.

Variations

⊚ Let a student hide the pennies.

⊚ Vary the locomotor skills, levels, pathways, and directions the students use while looking for the pennies.

⊚ Collaborative—Time the round. See whether the students can beat their best time in each new round.

⊚ Competitive—Let the students hold the pennies they collect. See which student collects the most pennies.

⊚ Let the students work in pairs, holding hands or linking arms.

⊚ Use something else that blends into the floor.

⊚ If you have a grassy outdoor area, try golf tees.

⊚ If the students are older, let them dribble a ball while looking for the pennies.

Far Away

Far Away is one of the best games for teaching young children how to take advantage of all the general space in the play area.

Topics

⊚ Aerobic endurance

⊚ Cooperation

⊚ Leadership skills

⊚ Spatial awareness

⊚ Safety awareness

Objectives

⊚ Psychomotor—Demonstrate several locomotor skills.

⊚ Cognitive—Be able to determine boundary lines and distances from each other.

⊚ Affective—Move safely and cooperate with children who are judging.

Equipment

None

Safety

⊚ Discuss the safety issue of moving into open spaces, keeping away from walls, benches, or other obstacles that may cause injury.

⊚ Move with control.

⊚ Look in the direction you are going.

⊚ Stay inside a perimeter line, such as the boundary line of a basketball court. If there are no lines, keep away from walls or benches.

Game

1. Students move throughout the play area using various locomotor skills. Ask the students how far away from each other they can move by going into the open spaces. If there is a perimeter line, they do not cross the line.

2. Select two or three students to act as judges for each round.

3. Begin by saying, "When I say to go, see whether you can (pick a different skill each time: jog, skip, hop, gallop, walk, leap, jump, slide, and so forth) throughout the play area, keeping inside the boundary line, and when I say to stop, can you freeze?" The judge or judges pick out a designated number of students who are farthest from everyone else and are not near a boundary line (the boundary line functions as if it were another student). These students become the new judges.

Variations

⊚ Use music as the start and stop signals.

⊚ Pick nouns and let the students interpret the movements.

⊚ Pick one student who is farthest away from everyone else. That student becomes the new judge. Each judge then picks a new judge after every round.

⊚ Let the judge decide what locomotor skill the group will perform.

⊚ You are the only judge. Give points for being far away.

⊚ Add equipment for more advanced students.

Fast Partners

This game encourages students to change partners quickly and work with many classmates.

Topics

⊚ Aerobic endurance

⊚ Locomotor skills

⊚ Cooperation

⊚ Spatial awareness

⊚ Safety awareness

Objectives

⊚ Psychomotor—Demonstrate several locomotor skills in pairs or groups.

⊚ Cognitive—Understand the need for moving safely; understand the need for being able to work with many different people.

⊚ Affective—Be willing to work with many different people; appreciate individual differences in ability.

Equipment

Music

Safety

⚠ Demonstrate how pairs move together safely without pulling or pushing.

Game

1. Using any number of creative ways, the students pair off.
2. While the music is on, the students join hands or link arms and skip throughout the play area.
3. When the music stops, the students drop hands and skip to a new partner. When the music begins again, the new partners begin skipping together. Stress the importance of working with many different people, and ensure that students change partners often.

Variations

⊚ Vary the locomotor skills.

⊚ Vary the direction, speed, pathway, or level.

⊚ Vary the number of students in each group. For example, have three or four students join together.

⊚ Vary the way the partners or groups join together. For example, have one partner hold the other's waist, with one in front and the other in back.

⊚ Use dance steps to move.

⊚ If holding hands is an issue, let the partners move close together without touching.

I'm Tired

Although this is a great warm-up game, it may be used as a complete game after the class has gained some aerobic fitness. Explain that the game will help make the students' hearts stronger.

Topics

⊚ Aerobic endurance

⊚ Locomotor skills

⊚ Cooperation

⊚ Safety awareness

Objectives

⊚ Psychomotor—Be able to move continuously for 2 to 5 minutes while demonstrating various locomotor skills.

- Cognitive—Recognize the various locomotor skills; know when the body needs a rest.
- Affective—Cooperate by moving safely throughout the play area.

Equipment

None, or a manipulative for each student (ages 7 and up)

Safety

- Move with control.
- Watch where you are going.

Game

1. Students spread out in scatter formation.
2. Introduce or review three or four locomotor skills. Some possibilities are sliding, skipping, jogging, and jumping.
3. The students practice these skills.
4. Establish an order for the three or four skills by saying, for example, "When I say to go, can you slide in any direction without touching anyone or anything; when I give the signal to change (any kind of verbal or audio signal), can you skip; at the next signal can you jog; at the next signal can you jump; and at the next signal can you go back to sliding?" The movement order remains the same.
5. Keep the game going for 2 to 5 minutes, or as long as the aerobic ability of the class allows. The amount of time between rest periods can increase progressively with each new lesson.
6. When a student feels tired, he walks slowly, raises his hand, and loudly announces, "I'm tired." The student may now rest by walking slowly until he feels better.
7. The student puts both hands up and says, "I feel fine," and immediately rejoins the game.

Variations

- Pick a leader to change movements at each signal. The leader can move in any of the given ways or create a new movement (running is not permitted). The students move the same way the leader is moving. Change leaders often.
- Use equipment for ages 7 and up.

Letter Cones

The students move throughout the play area while reinforcing their letter recognition.

Topics

- Aerobic endurance
- Locomotor skills
- Cooperation
- Letter recognition
- Sound recognition
- Safety awareness

Objectives

- Psychomotor—Demonstrate several locomotor skills at various levels, pathways, and speeds; interpret the way machines and animals move.
- Cognitive—Recognize all letters of the alphabet; know the sounds of all letters.
- Affective—Help each other; cooperate to keep the game moving and safe.

Equipment

- 1 cardboard letter for every student, each about 4 square inches (26 square centimeters) in size
- 1 traffic cone for each student

Safety

- Look in the direction you are going.
- Move with control so as not to bump into anyone or anything.

Game

1. Each student receives one traffic cone.
2. The students take their cones, find personal space, and stand or sit behind their cones.
3. Try several locomotor skills (walking, jogging, skipping, galloping, and so on). Ask the students to travel without touching each other or any of the cones. If they accidentally move or knock down a cone, they stop and fix it.

4. Give one letter to each student. Ask them to place the letter flat on top of their cone.

5. At the go signal (use music if possible), students take their letter and move the way an animal or machine that begins with that letter moves. If they cannot think of one, they hold the letter in front of them while walking. You or any other student may help them think of an animal or machine.

6. At the stop signal, the students freeze. Ask them to place their letter on top of anyone else's cone.

7. They then go back to their original cone to find a new letter. Continue in this manner.

Variations

⑥ Combine letters and make animal or machine words. All students who combine the letters to make a word move as that animal or machine moves.

⑥ Instead of using letters, place written instructions under each cone, such as *Walk like a penguin*. The students read the instructions, take the instructions with them, and move the way the instructions say. After each round, they place the instructions under a different cone.

⑥ Place letters on tennis balls or playground balls and substitute them for the cardboard ones. Students may also bounce the balls as they move.

Progressive Movement

This is an excellent game to see how many locomotor skills the students know and are able to do. Ages 4 to 6 will enjoy the pure movement. The older children can use a manipulative.

Topics

⑥ Aerobic endurance

⑥ Locomotor skills

⑥ Spatial awareness

⑥ Safety awareness

Objectives

⊚ Psychomotor—Be able to move in many ways, levels, and pathways.

⊚ Cognitive—Understand how to move efficiently.

⊚ Affective—Work cooperatively; understand how to be a leader and a follower.

Equipment

None, or a manipulative for each student (ages 7 and up)

Safety

Move with control and look for the open spaces.

Game

1. Ask the students to find personal space and stand in that space.

2. Choose one student to begin a locomotor skill.

3. That student chooses a locomotor skill and begins moving until she touches another student lightly on the shoulder.

4. The student whom she touched begins a different skill or chooses a different level or pathway. The first student now moves the same way as the student she just touched.

5. The two students move off in different directions, both moving in the same way, and choose two more students who once again change the skill. Now four students are moving.

6. The process continues until all students are moving. When everyone is moving, students continue their chosen locomotor skill for 1 to 2 minutes.

7. Students must watch the student they chose in order to be able to copy the movement, level, and pathway of the new movement.

Variations

⊚ All students move in a certain manner or pathway or at a certain level. For example, everyone skips diagonally backward.

⊚ The last student touched becomes the first student to begin the next round.

⊚ Give each student a manipulative. The students move and manipulate their pieces of equipment. The students try to copy the person they just touched.

Stay in the Boat

This action-packed game helps the students understand how to move throughout general space no matter how much space is available.

Topics

- Aerobic endurance
- Locomotor skills
- Cooperation
- Maximum use of general space

Objectives

- Psychomotor—Demonstrate at least four locomotor skills.
- Cognitive—Recognize that the same locomotor skill will look different when space is limited.
- Affective—Seek to move safely and cooperatively.

Equipment

None

Safety

- Move with control.
- Look in the direction you are going.
- Move inside the established boundary lines.

Game

1. Establish a boundary line around the play area. For example, use the perimeter of a basketball or volleyball court.
2. Students must stay inside the line. Any area inside the line is the boat, and any area outside the line is the ocean. If a student falls into the ocean, he earns a negative point. The idea is not to accumulate any points.
3. Ask the students to walk around the inside of the boat, keeping as far away from each other as they can but never going off the boat.
4. The students try other locomotor skills such as jogging, skipping, or jumping. As the students become more proficient at moving inside the boat, you can make the boat smaller or divide the group into two or three smaller boats, using lines in the gymnasium or tape lines on the floor (see figure 6.2). If lines are not available, poly spots can be used to mark off the boat area.

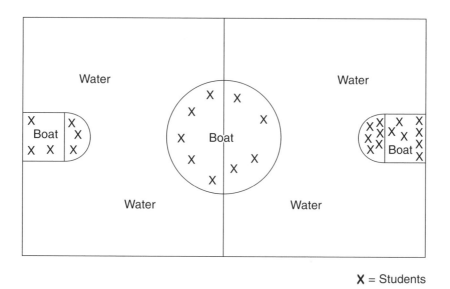

X = Students

Figure 6.2 Floor diagram for Stay in the Boat.

Variations

- Ask the students to go for a swim in the ocean. The students jump into the water and pretend to swim. They can try various swimming strokes. They can swim on the floor (low level) or swim standing up, moving their arms in a swimming motion (medium or high level).

- Ask the students to change boats with another group.

- Play music. When the music is on, the students are allowed to go swimming in the ocean, but when the music stops, the students quickly get back into their own boats.

- While the students are swimming in the water or changing boats, you become a shark. When you gently touch one of the swimmers, that student is considered eaten by the shark and earns a negative point. The idea is not to accumulate any points.

- More advanced students can manipulate equipment.

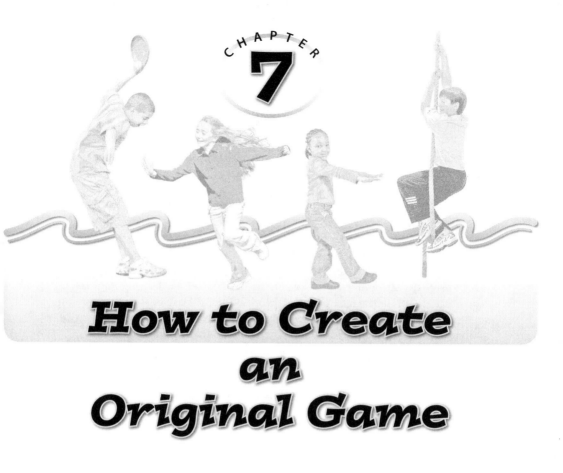

How to Create
an
Original Game

I magine two children out on their own, playing with a ball. They
might have fun for an hour simply playing catch. They might begin
to use their imaginations and try some variations. For example, one
might pretend to be a shortstop and the other a first-base player. The
first-base player throws a grounder to the shortstop, who picks it up
and throws to first for the imaginary out. After three outs, they switch
roles. Perhaps they decide to play a game of errors in which they try
to make their partner miss the ball. They might even make believe that
they are famous infielders or outfielders making great plays on the ball.
Although these children are having great fun and practicing skills, they
would likely become bored in a physical education class playing catch
unless you quickly either made catch into a game or instructed them to
invent their own game.

Have you noticed how often I have used points and time to organize
games? If you simply tell the children to count their total successful
catches in a given time limit or the most consecutive catches made in
a given time limit, you have created a simple game. After the time limit
they may see which pair scored the highest (competitive). They may try

to beat their best score with each ensuing round, working to better their own performance as well as assessing problems and tactics, or they may add up the entire class total and attempt to do better in the following rounds (cooperative). Now this drill of throwing and catching becomes an exciting game. If you want to add an element of fitness, you may ask the children to keep moving as they throw and catch (aerobic endurance).

Now that you have read and tried many of the games in this book, it is time to use the concepts you have learned to create your own original games. Always keep in mind that a game may not fully work the first time you play it. However, after playing the game you will be able to make the necessary adjustments to achieve your game playing goals.

Many ways exist to create an original game. Before beginning the process of creating an original game, decide what skill, fitness focus, or knowledge will be the game's focal point. Once the objective is clear, use the following eight guidelines to help create exciting original games that will maximize participation, movement, cooperation, and fun.

1. Change an existing game. For example, in the game Figure It Out the students sit in a circle and copy the movements of the leader, while someone else tries to guess who the leader is. The game Moving Figure It Out is created by asking all the students to move throughout general space while the leader constantly changes locomotor skills.

2. Modify one or more rules to improve participation and skill building or to add movement. For example, instead of playing traditional volleyball, allow the ball to bounce once, allow unlimited passes, allow only the forearm pass, play cooperative volleyball (any way that allows both teams to work together), or play Crazy Volleyball (the ball remains in play as long as it is not rolling).

3. Modify distances or heights to suit the players. Play minigames such as short court tennis. Set up hoops attached to strings as targets for shooting basketballs. The young, small, or less powerful student will be able to use the proper shooting technique.

4. Add extra equipment. Two additional soccer goals and three additional soccer balls transform ordinary soccer into the exciting new game of Four Corner Soccer.

5. Use the maximum amount of equipment available. A game becomes more exciting to participants when they have something to manipulate and do not have to wait a long time for a chance. In the old game of Steal the Bacon, two teams line up and each student must wait most of the period to have one or two chances to perform.

The children who are not actually trying to steal the Indian club (bacon) cheer, watch, or perhaps lose interest and become bored or restless. Instead, use more Indian clubs scattered throughout the playing area, with each small group of five to nine players having their own club and one leftover player (students take turns) calling the numbers. This structure transforms the game into a very active one. In addition, the students get the additional advantage of learning to lead a game.

6. Play small-group games. Rather than playing a large game like line soccer, play a small-group game like Triangle and Two. This is a simple game in which three players form a triangle and pass the ball to each other, while the other two attempt to intercept the ball.

7. De-emphasize winning and losing. The goals of cooperation, learning, and fun are primary to successful game playing. Winning very often takes one or all of these goals away from the game. How often have carefully taught skills broken down during a regulation game of soccer or basketball?

8. Get ideas from popular TV shows, movies, books, board games, or toys. For example, instead of playing Read and Do (see page 16 for game description), play Charlotte's Web. In this game, sketch a large web on cardboard. This is Charlotte's Web. The children in the class are all Wilbur. You (the teacher) are Charlotte (or maybe Charlie). When Charlotte holds a word up next to the web, all the Wilburs do what the word says.

Most games fit into certain categories. Here is a descriptive list of the main categories

1. Tag or dodgeball (similar to tag, but with a ball)—These are chasing and fleeing games of various kinds:
   - Progressive—One person begins as the It. Each person tagged joins the Its until everyone is tagged.
   - Joining a group—One person begins as the It. Each person tagged joins hands until everyone becomes part of the group.
   - Prisoner—Team tag in which the tagged person becomes a prisoner or joins the other team.
   - Infinity—A version that allows the tagged person to get back in the game.
2. Team goals or points as in basketball, soccer, or volleyball

3. Individual goals or points as in bowling, tennis, or archery

4. Races—Contests for getting from one point to another; may be individual (timed), relay, group, or partners

5. Judged competition, as in skating or gymnastics

6. Guessing games, as in Figure It Out or Concentration

7. Following directions, as in orienteering or movement questions

8. Hiding and finding, as in Hide and Seek or finding hidden objects

Combine the guidelines and the categories to create an original game. In addition, mix and match guidelines and categories. The following is an example of creating a game from start to finish:

1. I want to create a game that will help the students improve their ability to set (overhand pass) a volleyball.

2. Following the above guidelines, I divide the class into groups of six to eight players and give each group three or four volleyballs. If I have volleyball trainers, I use them in upper elementary grades and perhaps even in middle school. I can further modify the equipment by using beach balls, slow-motion balls, or balloons.

3. I want the group to have fun and concentrate on the skill but not worry about winning or losing.

4. I know a game called Team Juggling. In this game, a group passes a ball back and forth across a circle until everyone in the circle has had one chance. The last person to receive the ball passes it back to the person who began the sequence. After children practice the same sequence until the passing becomes smooth and everyone knows whom to pass to, the first person adds a second ball to the rotation. Eventually a third or fourth ball may be added.

5. I modify this game to include setting a volleyball. A less skilled group may set the ball and allow the next person to catch it before setting it. A more skilled group may try to continuously set the ball from one person to the next. Thus a new game is created. We can call this game Set Pass Juggling.

6. I can have students play the same game as basketball or soccer by changing the equipment.

7. I can add an element of aerobic fitness by requiring the passer to move to a new location after each pass.

8. I can inject an element of TV by calling the game (Name of school) Idol Volleyball. In order to become the school idol, each group must show great coordination.

Finally, when creating an original game, try anything that may increase interest and fun or that changes the teaching focus. Then continue to modify it until the game achieves its goal.

About the Author

Howie Weiss, MA, is a staff developer for the New York City Department of Education. He taught physical education for over 30 years, served as a mentor for other teachers, and was the chairperson of the New York City physical education curriculum design team. Weiss has led workshops at local, state, and national physical education conferences. He received the Master Teacher Award from the New York Board of Education and is one of only 6 physical educators in New York City to ever receive this award. Weiss is a member of the American Association for Health, Physical Education, Recreation and Dance and the New York State Association for Health, Physical Education, Recreation and Dance.